Glynne Evans

Responding to Crises in the African Great Lakes

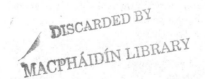
Adelphi Paper 311

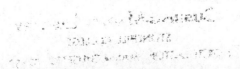

Oxford University Press, Great Clarendon Street, Oxford OX2 6DP
Oxford New York
Athens Auckland Bangkok Bombay Calcutta Cape Town
Dar es Salaam Delhi Florence Hong Kong Istanbul Karachi
Kuala Lumpur Madras Madrid Melbourne Mexico City
Nairobi Paris Singapore Taipei Tokyo Toronto
and associated companies in
Berlin Ibadan

Oxford is a trade mark of Oxford University Press

Published in the United States
by Oxford University Press Inc., New York

© The International Institute for Strategic Studies 1997

First published August 1997 by **Oxford University Press** for
The International Institute for Strategic Studies
23 Tavistock Street, London WC2E 7NQ
http://www.isn.ethz.ch/iiss

Director John Chipman
Deputy Director Rose Gottemoeller
Editor Gerald Segal
Assistant Editor Rachel Neaman
Design and Production Mark Taylor

British Library Cataloguing in Publication Data
Data available

Library of Congress Cataloguing in Publication Data

ISBN 0-19-829403-4
ISSN 0567-932x

contents

5   **List of maps**

7   **Introduction**

19 Chapter 1   **Identity and Insecurity**
    - *Political and Social Background 19*
    - *The Barundi Political Experiment 24*
    - *A Balance of Fear 26*
    - *The Collective Response: International Organisations 27*
    - *The Collective Response: The Sub-regional Role 33*
    - *Track-Two Action: The NGO Contribution 39*
    - *The Impact of Collective Action 41*

45 Chapter 2   **External Military Intervention Versus Local Action**
    - *Proposals for Protection 51*
    - *Preventive Deployment 56*
    - *Humanitarian Operations 62*
    - *Military Intervention Versus Political Reality 71*

77 **Conclusions**
- *Lessons and Proposals 79*
- *Conclusion 85*

87 **Notes**

maps

10   **Map 1**
      Central Africa and the Great Lakes Region

47   **Map 2**
      Rwanda and Burundi

History reveals that those caught up in revolutionary change rarely
understand its significance
Former UN Secretary-General Boutros Boutros-Ghali, 1996

Introduction

Western policy-makers can ill afford to ignore internal conflicts in remote states. Such conflicts have a capacity to fester and to surprise, to draw in neighbouring states and to destabilise an entire sub-region. From Bosnia to Burundi, these hostilities have in common major human-rights abuses and large-scale civilian suffering. Pictures of carnage, of traumatised children cradling AK-47s, and of seven-digit refugee movements are transmitted instantly around the world.[1] Such dramatic reporting of suffering can generate an emotional response in its audience, leading to public appeals for dramatic interventions.[2]

Many political analysts argue that intra-state conflict is the pattern of the times, and that it presents a serious threat to regional as well as national security and will continue to do so for the foreseeable future.[3] Neighbouring states become involved in these conflicts in a number of ways. They are obliged to give shelter to refugees, they provide transit routes for economic essentials, and they can facilitate or deny arms supplies. When ethnic links transcend formal boundaries, the spill over is even more destabilising, not only for immediate neighbours, but also for the entire sub-region. Violent social conflict within a state is dangerous, complex and does not respond to quick solutions.[4] There is much debate about the resolution of such conflicts, but little accord on their nature and root causes, or on the appropriate mix of policies for prevention or immediate response. A host of definitions and prescriptions from academics and policy-makers abound, from Africa to the Balkans.[5]

While practitioners and political analysts have sustained an effective dialogue on peacekeeping, the dynamics and complexities of violent social conflict within a state as analysed by the social scientist have not yet informed diplomatic or military thinking sufficiently. The essential links between practitioners and academics, so well structured during the Cold War, have yet to be forged in the less well-known area of internal conflict.[6] The responses familiar in East–West conflict management may not be appropriate for internal conflict within the Organisation for Security and Cooperation in Europe (OSCE) area, let alone for Africa.[7]

In the crises in Africa from 1993–97, an effective toolbox for policy response had not yet evolved. Practitioners, often ill-informed and usually under severe time pressure, had to cope with a complex and fast-moving situation. Dramatic developments on the ground were matched by escalating rhetoric and a proliferation of mediators. In early 1997, for example, there were 13 different negotiators in Burundi alone. When the rebellion in eastern Zaire (now the Democratic Republic of Congo, or DROC) became a real threat to former President Mobutu Sese Seko in 1997, the assortment of international players and interested parties, and the declarations of concern, burgeoned.[8] The final outcome, however, was precipitated from within Africa itself.

This paper examines the international responses to the ethnic conflict in Burundi and Rwanda from 1993–97 and its overspill into neighbouring Zaire. The main focus of the paper is Burundi, little analysed and little understood. Rwanda has already been the subject of a more detailed evaluation.[9] The study traces the interaction of both successive and parallel external attempts at mediation and conflict management with local initiatives. Chapter 1 uses the case study of Burundi to illustrate the nature of the conflict, the interaction with the wider sub-region and the varied and ultimately ineffective political responses of Western governments. Chapter 2 analyses the unproductive proposals made by external actors for military intervention in Burundi and eastern Zaire, and traces the background to the action by local forces that culminated in Mobutu's fall in May 1997.

This paper deals with the period from the assassination of Burundian President Melchior Ndadaye in October 1993 to the collapse of the Mobutu regime in June 1997. In Rwanda, Burundi and eastern Zaire, violent domestic conflict was generated by politicians deliberately using ethnicity and fear to mobilise support.[10] Every fresh episode of Hutu–Tutsi violence in Rwanda or Burundi provoked an outflow of refugees to neighbouring states. Refugee camps became a breeding ground for revanchism. The murder of President Ndadaye and the end of the democratic experiment in Burundi in 1993 exemplified the ethnic tensions within the country and the sub-region as a whole. The

politicians used ethnicity and fear to mobilise support

genocide in Rwanda in 1994 was a manifestation of the same deliberately manufactured violence. The rebellion in eastern Zaire in late 1996 began as a further instalment in the troubled Hutu–Tutsi relationship, but changed in nature as it developed.

Although the conflicts within Burundi and Rwanda, and later Zaire, provoked major international concern, they were difficult for outsiders to understand and even more difficult for them to deal with. Political and economic, military and humanitarian facets folded into one another in kaleidoscopic fashion. The West was shocked by reports of human-rights abuses that escalated into massacres, genocide and mass migration. The Hutu genocide in Rwanda and the killing in Burundi exceeded the mortality rate of any other conflict (Cambodia apart) since the Second World War. In Rwanda, estimates range from 500,000–800,000 deaths in 1994. In Burundi, the accumulated death toll in successive violent episodes between 1993 and 1997 was believed to be at least 150,000.[11] Eastern Zaire took the burden of the civilian Hutu migration from Rwanda after the genocide in 1994. The UN High Commission for Refugees (UNHCR) reluctantly ran the camps that accommodated the refugees and the Hutu extremists who had orchestrated the genocide. In these camps, Hutu militias were armed, trained and prepared to take back Rwanda, with the complicity of the Mobutu regime. The collapse of these camps to Zairean rebel forces in late 1996 revealed a sophisticated network of arms suppliers and detailed plans for invading Rwanda.[12]

Significantly, the fall of the Mobutu regime in May 1997 was precipitated by a rebellion sparked by sub-regional developments moving in from Zaire's eastern borders, not by political collapse in the capital, Kinshasa. A localised reaction to racism in eastern Zaire

Map I *Central Africa and the Great Lakes Region*

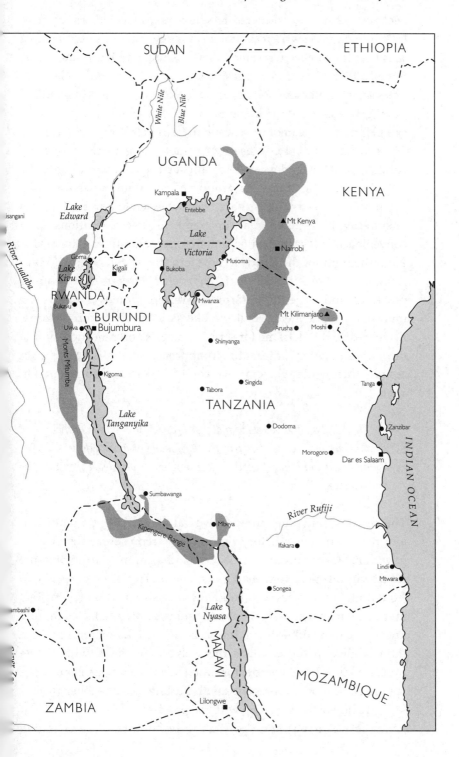

became a skilfully conducted rebellion that revealed starkly how little influence the writ of central government had outside Kinshasa. This bore the intellectual stamp of other similar military campaigns, notably that of Ugandan President Yoweri Museveni's National Resistance Movement (NRM) in 1984–86 – supported by his then intelligence chief, Paul Kagame – and of Kagame's own classic campaign at the head of the Rwandan Patriotic Front (RPF) in 1994.

When ethnicity is used as a mobilising force in internal conflict, political leaders seek to gain support by presenting to the outside world an image of group suffering among the civilian community.[13] Western states have been subjected to powerful images of suffering by virtue of real-time reporting and a 'relationship of convenience' between the humanitarian community and the media. From the flight of the Kurds in northern Iraq to the plight of Hutu refugees in Zaire in 1996 and 1997, relief workers can secure a powerful and urgent platform in Western homes through the immediacy of the media. Policy-makers are thus left with a dramatically reduced timeframe for serious analysis and reflection, and to develop a coherent international approach to a crisis.[14] As Kofi Annan, then Under-Secretary-General for Peacekeeping, stated in 1996:

> *The 'CNN factor' tends to mobilise pressure at the peak of the problem – which is to say, at the very moment when effective intervention is most costly, most dangerous and least likely to succeed.*[15]

The all-consuming and competitive nature of real-time reporting, and the often contradictory reports from representatives of non-governmental organisations (NGOs) on the ground, create pressure for a swift response to distant emergencies. This often gives rise to 'soundbite' diplomacy and sudden policy shifts, as policy-makers make statements and accelerate decisions before the facts are fully known.[16] On the other hand, the absence of media pictures and the intractability of the conflicts themselves, combined with a new problem elsewhere, could cause a crisis to disappear from international attention, as happened with Burundi after October 1996.

Policy-makers dealing with the problems of the African Great Lakes between 1993 and 1997 had to respond to a fast-changing scene and to scenarios they could not easily understand. That civil war had become well-planned genocide in Rwanda in 1994 was hard to comprehend. It also took time to detect the mix of skilful opportunism and local security concerns that caused an isolated rebellion in eastern Zaire – which dealt brutally with the long-running problem of the overcrowded Hutu refugee camps in October 1996 – to progress to a march on the capital in May 1997. Rwandan, Ugandan and even Angolan local security concerns became part of a further-reaching African-led political and geostrategic vision, executed decisively and even violently.[17] Although Burundi had been in crisis in July 1996 following the military coup against President Sylvestre Ntibantunganya, the difficulties of access by humanitarian organisations and the media, combined with the intractability of its problems, meant that it virtually disappeared from international view. Given the complexity of, and pace at which, internal conflict and sub-regional instability developed in an area little known to them, Western practitioners anxious to respond to the crises – whether for reasons of stability or humanitarianism – had little opportunity to draw practical or conceptual policy lessons from academic writing, or even to draw on the experience of specialist NGOs.[18]

The United Nations, the Organisation of African Unity (OAU), African statesmen singly and collectively, Western envoys, a former US President and NGOs all came forward and then retreated as a range of policies was tried. In Rwanda and Burundi, as in Bosnia, experience proved the difficulty of applying the tools valued in inter-state disputes to warring entities operating at sub-state level. Arms embargoes, sanctions and declaratory warnings lose their force when neighbouring states are prepared to turn a blind eye. A donor's promise to give – or threat to withhold – financial support has considerable impact on a state, but less on a faction that is still remote from power or independently financed, and presents difficult moral choices in an aid-dependent country. Once ethnicity has been deliberately used by local politicians to fuel a conflict that is essentially about control of and access to resources, short-term solutions based on cease-fires and sketchy peace agreements are not viable. External power projection and military intervention on an impartial humanitarian basis are difficult concepts in ethnic conflict. In a war between citizens, the motivation can be intensely local.[19]

The international proposals for external military intervention in Burundi, Rwanda or eastern Zaire, almost all without a clear objective or political strategy, in part reflected the difficulty of establishing an effective or even a common political ground for action. These proposals, and the half-hearted military planning that went into them, were evidence of the guilt felt by the international community over the genocide in Rwanda, rather than viable options. Then UN Secretary-General Boutros Boutros-Ghali received no support for his proposal to send an enforcement mission to Rwanda in 1994, nor to deploy a stand-by force in Zaire to prevent genocide in Burundi in 1995. Tanzanian-led plans for military assistance to Burundi in mid-1996 gave way instead to sub-regional sanctions against President Pierre Buyoya's regime in July. The *ad hoc* Multi-national Force (MNF) proposed in November 1996 to save refugees in eastern Zaire had already collapsed by December, and resisted attempts at resuscitation in March 1997. The message became clear. Mixed political objectives in the West meant divided counsels. A Western intervention to 'save lives' divorced from a coherent political strategy was not a sufficient cause; a clear lesson from the Bosnia experience. Moreover, recognition of the difficulty of devising a valid concept of military operations for Burundi without taking sides, or for eastern Zaire without playing into the political game of whether or not the Mobutu regime survived, meant that the only deployment (peacekeeping in Rwanda apart) was a small mission of OAU observers in Burundi between 1994 and 1996. An ephemeral multi-national headquarters was also established in Entebbe to back up the intended, but in fact non-existent, MNF in Zaire – where bored soldiers occupied themselves playing with monkeys[20] – and various short-term deployments to evacuate Western nationals in times of open conflict.

> *Western intervention to 'save lives' was not a sufficient cause*

A major theme to emerge from the successive crises in the African Great Lakes was the power of local, rather than inter-national, action both to set the agenda and to provide the solution. Proposals for a cease-fire to halt the conflict without adequate recognition of the military and political realities, or for neutral and humanitarian intervention between parties, did not prosper. Indeed, Alain Destexhe, former Secretary-General of *Médecins sans Frontières* (MSF), argued that the UN should have taken sides in 1994 as soon as it became clear that the former Rwandan government was carrying out genocide. The columnist William Pfaff has further argued that external intervention can make things worse and 'can sometimes prolong suffering by temporarily blocking events from reaching their necessary conclusion'.[21] It was the swift victory of the Tutsi-dominated RPF that ended the Hutu extremist campaign of genocide in Rwanda in 1994; it was neighbouring African states that imposed sanctions on Burundi's Buyoya regime following the overthrow of President Ntibantunganya in July 1996; and it was non-governmental players that provided the only route to peace in Burundi in 1997. Attacks by Zairean rebels and their allies, not multinational action, closed the refugee camps in 1996, and Zaire's own future was decided by a local rebellion with sub-regional support, rather than by the political plan laid down by the US, France and Belgium in 1993, or the 1997 US–South African–UN-sponsored peace negotiations. Although humanitarian drama peaked in the West, it did not change local dynamics. In Burundi, external pressures had no result – regional sanctions benefited the Tutsi élite, and the EU's declaratory policy had no real impact. Informal activity by track-two players, however, began to re-engage the political class in 1997 in a process which offered some potential.

A number of lessons emerge:

- violent social conflict within a state, and its impact on its neighbours, is brutish, and superficial responses do not produce lasting solutions;
- understanding the causes and dynamics of such conflicts is essential in considering a response;
- competition between international players and the power of the media image transmitted in real time have foreshortened the time available for decision-making – to which governments and institutions need to adapt;
- solutions are more likely to come from within the internal political process than from without; and
- military choices are starker than hitherto believed, and the neutral option requires a heavy and durable commitment.

Applying pressure, whether sanctions or the threat of military force, is futile unless all these dynamics are understood. Indeed, a military intervention will interfere with local dynamics – often complicating and protracting a situation rather than simplifying it – unless the aim is indeed to change the correlation of local factions and impose a solution by force. In Africa at least, a local solution may go against the grain of international activism, but may be more effective and lasting. Local solutions that involve substantial human-rights abuses, however, tend to store up violence for the future.

A direct contribution to promoting a more effective international response to internal conflicts and small wars would be for the UN to create a Conflict Analysis Centre (CAC) in New York as an acknowledged centre of excellence. This would reposition the UN at the heart of international activity in conflict management, even as its former role in peacekeeping is increasingly shared with other organisations. The CAC would be tasked with examining the roots of conflict, drawing out lessons learned and providing a sound analytical base for further action. Such work would have practical relevance for conflict prevention and management, and would help to limit the institutional competition that has been so marked during the 1990s.[22] Governments need a more sophisticated approach to conflict management, not least in promoting lateral understanding and cooperation between the different players, whether the diplomatic service, the media or the NGO community. Multicultural training in peacekeeping and conflict management between practitioners of different disciplines, as pioneered by the UK in exercises run jointly by the Foreign and Commonwealth Office and the Army Staff College at Camberley will remain an essential part of this work.[23] Norway, for its part, has an enviable record in promoting both track-one and track-two activities and offers a valuable model for others, not least in its Foreign Ministry's ability to provide funds swiftly and discreetly, as it did to both Burundi and the Middle East.

the UN should create a Conflict Analysis Centre

Writers of military doctrine need to bring out the peculiarly nasty nature of domestic conflict and make clear that the choice lies between taking sides if a short-term solution is required, or protracted commitment if the aim is to protect the vulnerable against the aggressor within the same society. Human-rights monitoring and effective means to publicise abuse where it occurs remain vital. Finally, the West and the global international institutions need to design a framework for economic cooperation and assistance at the sub-regional level in the African Great Lakes. In this way, they could encourage political progress on the political side and longer-term reconciliation.

The Heads of State and delegations call upon the international community
to condemn vigorously the ethnic and political genocide ideology used in
competition for conquest and monopoly of power [in Rwanda and Burundi].
Declaration of the Heads of State and Government of the African
Great Lakes Region, Cairo, 29 November 1995

As soon as a man has surrendered himself
to the crowd, he ceases to fear its touch.
Elias Canetti, *Crowds and Power*

chapter 1

Identity and Insecurity

Political and Social Background

Since 1994, Rwanda has been indissolubly linked with genocide. Its neighbour, Burundi, has also been associated with a high and continuing level of violence. The tragedy of both lies in population pressures, a vicious interaction of events between the two countries that eventually involved neighbouring Zaire as well, and the calculated use over the past 30 years of ethnicity as an instrument of political mobilisation.

Polarisation of the two main ethnic groups – the Hutu and the Tutsi – dates from the period prior to Rwanda's independence in July 1962, and from the 1960s in Burundi. This polarisation is neither natural nor 'age-old'.[1] Instead, intermarriage between the two groups was widespread and there were clear economic and social rankings within both Tutsi and Hutu communities. It took time and application to create the divisions and the myths that now surround both groups. From the late 1950s onwards, the political élite in both Rwanda and Burundi used ethnicity in their struggle for power and state resources.[2] They also used violence as a means of promoting 'ethnic' group consciousness. From the 1970s onwards, each new episode in the history of Hutu–Tutsi violence strengthened the negative perceptions, however distorted, each side had of the other.

This background explains in part the extraordinary difficulties faced in the late 1990s by outside negotiators in dealing with the psychological as well as the political complexity of the African Great Lakes region.[3] Indeed, Ahmedou Ould Abdallah, the UN Special

Representative of the Secretary-General (SRSG) in Burundi from 1993–95, claimed that he needed an army of psychiatrists more than an army of blue-helmeted peacekeepers.[4]

Both Rwanda and Burundi are tiny, over-populated and poor states. Rwanda has an area of 26,000 square kilometres and Burundi 28,000. Before the 1994 genocide, Rwanda's population was 7.5 million and Burundi's 6m, giving a population density of 260–300 people per square kilometre, the highest in Africa. In the words of one analyst:

> *One need not be an impenitent Malthusian to realise that neither state can sustain the current pressures on their land without recourse to further violent 'readjustments'.*[5]

Gross domestic product (GDP) per head in 1995 was $290 in Rwanda and $259 in Burundi. The successive waves of violence between 1993 and 1996 destroyed the bases of these two already aid-dependent economies. Yet during this period neither qualified as a failed state, since the wheels of government continued to turn.

Group identity had been reinforced during Belgian colonial rule, and even after both countries gained their independence in July 1962, the ethnic balance in the two states remained roughly the same: 85% Hutu, 14% Tutsi and 1% Twa (or pygmy). In Rwanda in the colonial period, the Tutsi minority received priority in education and made up the governing élite, while the majority Hutu – largely agricultural peasants – were badly educated, deprived of political power and exploited by the colonial power and the Tutsi alike. From the late 1950s, however, largely under pressure from the Catholic Church, this trend was reversed and the principle of democracy based on majority was adopted. By the time political parties were formally established in the late 1950s, they followed ethnic lines. In 1959, a Hutu rebellion toppled Rwanda's Tutsi monarchy, and in elections in 1961, Hutu parties secured 83% of the vote. The minority Tutsi in turn became the second-class citizens.

In Burundi, polarisation on ethnic lines took longer than in Rwanda, since the divisions were more caste-based and the king and governing princely (or *Ganwa*) élite continued to play a role. The murder of Prince Rwagasore in October 1961, following his victory as head of the Union for National Progress (UPRONA) in legislative elections, was the first in a series of crises that led to ethnic division. From disputes that began within the *Ganwa* élite, the Hutu–Tutsi divide assumed increasing importance. With great prescience, a leading Hutu army officer (later to be murdered) remarked in 1961:

> *The evil comes from the top. It is the insatiable people in responsible positions who make political strategy out of ethnic divisions in order to further their shameful ambitions.*[6]

From 1959, violence followed every major political development in Rwanda and Burundi alike and provoked a fresh outflow of refugees. The Hutu revolt in Rwanda in 1959, the assassination of Prince Rwagasore in Burundi in 1961, the massacres and purges of the Hutu middle class in 1972 which helped consolidate Tutsi supremacy in Burundi, the killing of Tutsi following the coup by Juvénal Habyarima in Rwanda in 1973 and the brutal crushing of an anti-Tutsi uprising in Burundi in 1988 were all watersheds. By the 1980s, some 480,000 Rwandan Tutsi (about half the indigenous Tutsi community), had taken refuge in neighbouring countries, with 280,000 in Burundi alone. By 1991, 240,000 Hutu had fled from Burundi.[7] These refugee communities fuelled rumour, violence and revanchism.

Since the late 1960s, ethnic tension in Burundi has been high, and the Hutu and the Tutsi systematically demonised each other further with each violent episode. The Tutsi fostered the fear that the demographic majority would murder the minority – what they termed the 'Hutu peril'. The Hutu, for their part, believed that the Tutsi would attempt to restore numerical balance by killing the Hutu. Each side thus preyed on a fear of the future while promulgating a myth-

Hutu and Tutsi systematically demonised each other

ical representation of the past, creating a widespread culture of insecurity and terror.[8] SRSG Ould Abdallah argues that each death or massacre of either side was intended not only to kill an individual, but also to destroy part of the entire Hutu or Tutsi ethnic group.[9]

By the 1970s, killing was presented as all but a civic duty. Burundi's Tutsi government encouraged the population in radio broadcasts to 'hunt down the python in the grass', an order interpreted by the Tutsi population as licence to exterminate all educated Hutu, down to children at secondary – and in some cases even primary – school. Army units commandeered lorries and removed whole batches of schoolchildren from their classes at a time. Tutsi pupils even prepared lists of their Hutu classmates to facilitate identification by officials.[10] Up to 300,000 Hutu perished in the pogroms of 1972.

The regime of Colonel Jean Baptiste Bagaza in 1967–87 intensified Tutsi domination. Tutsi Major Pierre Buyoya, who took power from Bagaza in a bloodless coup in 1987, initially followed his predecessor's policy, but adopted a reformist line after the Hutu uprising and its brutal repression in August 1988. Lemarchand describes the 1988 events as a 'sudden outburst of rage, followed by intense fears of an impending re-enactment of the 1972 carnage'.[11] Hutu refugees, newly arrived in Rwanda, explained that the violence, which left 5,000 dead and 10,000 homeless, had been prompted by unannounced army manoeuvres, which led to fears of an impending Tutsi-led massacre. Thus the Hutu had begun to kill pre-emptively, and the army had responded brutally. By late 1996, the UN Commission of Enquiry, set up the previous year to investigate the 1993 assassination of President Ndadaye, found that all-embracing ethnic confrontation was not confined to the political class and the military, but permeated every layer of society: 'it was an inescapable fact that the overwhelming majority of Burundians considered themselves to belong to one or other group'. Ethnic consciousness and hunger for land could and did lead peaceful Hutu farmers to participate in the massacre of their neighbours.[12]

Fear and insecurity consistently promoted violence. The culture of fear was fed not only by the refugee camps across the border in Zaire, but also by the Hutu leadership in Rwanda. Speaking from a place of exile with the RPF in 1993, Hutu Pasteur Bizimungu, who became Prime Minister of Rwanda following the RPF victory in 1994, commented:

> *The Kigali regime has persistently taken advantage of what has happened in Burundi. Instead of helping them unite, it*

has invited them to fight one another. The decision of the Rwandan government to support the government in exile is one of the steps intended to divide Burundians instead of helping them to solve their current problems. Radio Rwanda instead of uniting our brothers has insisted on broadcasting rumour. This has led to people going for one another's throats. The same radio kept asking Burundi citizens to protect themselves. On closer examination, they were not telling them to oppose those who were armed, but were telling them to kill one another, as became clear later.[13]

By 1990, selective killing was part of the common coinage of politics. Hutu and Tutsi armed groups had multiplied, with civilians their main target. Amnesty International noted that it was often difficult to tell which group had committed a specific murder or human-rights abuse. Only the ethnic identity of the victim offered a clue.[14] At a meeting in Cairo in November 1995, African sub-regional heads of state condemned the ethnic and political genocide ideology used in both countries to win power.[15]

killing was part of the common coinage of politics

And with violence went impunity. No-one had punished or even condemned the massacres of 1972. SRSG Ould Abdallah and the Prosecutor for the UN International Criminal Tribunals, Judge Richard Goldstone, both regarded the culture of impunity allowed by the Bujumbura government as a major factor in continuing violence and genocide. The UN Special Rapporteur for Human Rights Sergio Pinheiro, and the UN Commission of Enquiry into the murder of President Ndadaye took the same view.[16]

Professional diplomats regarded as hyperbole the demonic vision set out in April 1995 by Burundi's Permanent Representative to the UN in a letter to the Security Council:

The Tutsi are afraid of being wiped out altogether and recall with horror the massacres in Burundi in October and November 1993 and the recent genocide against the Tutsi in Rwanda. The Hutu believe that the Tutsi helped by the 'Tutsi-dominated' army are going to avenge their kin who were massacred in 1993.[17]

Never can there have been so clear an example of the dangers of crowd psychosis and the need to exorcise the fear of being murdered, as described by Nobel Laureate Elias Canetti.[18] In February 1996, UN Secretary-General Boutros-Ghali outlined a political and security situation in the region defined by visceral fears and brutal power struggles:

> *Most of the Tutsi minority, historically dominant, live with the phobia of its political elimination, while the Hutu majority demands proper political representation. The 1994 genocide in Rwanda has heightened the fears of the minority, leading extremist elements to undertake ruthless actions against Hutu populations. Hutu extremists in turn are reinforced and supported from outside the country by some of the perpetrators of the Rwandan genocide. In such an environment, the voices of moderation are being drowned out or eliminated altogether.[19]*

This analysis was first class, but it somehow seemed to get lost. From late 1994, Boutros-Ghali had appeared to recommend all options at the same time – political, military, economic and humanitarian – lest he be faulted. Sensible steps, such as strengthening the judicial system, were inevitably overshadowed by recommendations for military action which looked robust, but were neither politically nor practically viable.

The Barundi Political Experiment

International fears that the 1994 genocide in Rwanda might be repeated in Burundi were palpable. Despite its fragile domestic situation, however, Burundi did not explode into systematic genocidal violence as it had in 1972. The reason for this lies in the distinct evolution of Burundian politics. From 1989–93, during the second half of Buyoya's first term as President, the prospect of building lasting political structures designed by the Barundi themselves was raised.[20]

Legislative elections in Burundi in June 1993 were the culmination of a reform process, and an apparent retreat from the politics of ethnic mobilisation, launched in 1989 by Buyoya. Initially, there was little to distinguish Buyoya from previous Tutsi authoritarian rulers. But the government's so-called 'law-and-order operations' in August 1988 against Hutu elements provoked a strong international reaction. By 1988, principles of good governance in the international community had a much higher profile, and human-rights abuses and military coups were no longer tolerated. The US Congress urged then President Ronald Reagan to press for a 'negotiated non-violent reform of Burundi's historical inequities', to reassess US relations with Burundi, and to suspend US aid unless the Buyoya regime introduced internal reforms and ended ethnic discrimination.[21]

International pressure from Canada, the European Community, the US and the World Bank, exerted via threats to suspend aid, had a salutary effect and Buyoya changed tack. Ethnic divisions were admitted and 'national unity' entered the domestic lexicon for the first time. The President launched a national debate to seek views from all sectors of society, and set up a national commission to draft a Charter of National Unity that was published in 1990. Education and the civil service were opened to the Hutu, but not the army or the judiciary. Buyoya called elections for 1993 and, deliberately seeking to promote a multi-party approach, encouraged the formation of political parties that transcended ethnic divisions. A new liberal Constitution was approved in a referendum by 90% of the people of Burundi on 9 March 1993. Presidential elections were held on 1 June 1993, and parliamentary elections on 29 June.

Buyoya's promotion of a multi-party system alarmed politicians on both sides. The Front for Democracy in Burundi (FRODEBU) was founded in March 1993 by Melchior Ndadaye and other Hutu intellectuals. It immediately attracted support from the Hutu élite as the party to end Tutsi rule. As the Hutu mobilised politically, the Tutsi accused FRODEBU of being an ethnic organisation and feared that its success would institutionalise Hutu domination, as in

Buyoya's promotion of a multi-party system alarmed politicians on both sides

Rwanda. The more FRODEBU was identified with Hutuism by its opponents, the more it appeared attractive as a promoter and defender of the interests of the demographic majority against constant Tutsi violence. For their part, the Tutsi-led UPRONA founded the youth militia *Sans Echec* which was to play a malevolent role in mobilising and coordinating youth demonstrations and violence on the streets in the crises that followed.

Buyoya's courage and vision, and indeed his own Hutu family connections through his mother's second marriage, only barely overcame ethnic divisions. In the June presidential elections, he secured 32% of the vote, while Ndadaye polled 64.5%. The outcome of the parliamentary elections more closely reflected the ethnic mix. FRODEBU won 71.4% of the votes cast and 65 of the 81 seats in the Assembly, and UPRONA 21.4% of the votes.[22] Buyoya, who had expected victory, took defeat gracefully and stressed that it was the first time that a Burundian president had taken over from his predecessor democratically on the basis of the country's laws and Constitution, a step that earned Burundi international respect. In handing over power, he thanked President-elect Ndadaye for promising to pursue the policy of national unity. Buyoya stressed the importance of working for the whole society. He recalled that in a democracy, any competitors must abide by the population's will. He said now that the elections are over, the winners have to work for the welfare of the whole society. They have to celebrate their victory without threatening the losers or leading to the nation's fall.[23] Ndadaye expressed similar sentiments, saying that the way to a new Burundi was justice for all, sharing and tolerance:

> Today, both the losers and the winners have to join together to share the joy of the victory which brings freedom; all have to recognise that they are Barundi and that they are equal in front of the law.[24]

A Balance of Fear

In Burundi, however, Hutu–Tutsi divisions were now formalised politically. The inauguration of President Ndadaye on 10 July was a visible symbol of Hutu dominance in perpetuity. Three years later, Pie Masumbuko, a founder member of UPRONA, expressed the Tutsi perception:

> A numerical majority of Hutus over Tutsis is not democracy. If democracy puts Hutus in power, that is tribalism. One man one vote means nothing here.[25]

But if the Hutu controlled the political institutions, the Tutsi still controlled the Burundian Army. As a Tutsi journalist explained to a foreign commentator in Bujumbura:

> *Don't think of it as a typical army; think of it as the Tutsi-extermination deterrent force.*[26]

The attempted military coup against the government in October 1993 was a dividing line. It established a balance of fear between the predominantly Tutsi army and the Hutu demographic majority. Ethnicity again became paramount, overriding all other considerations. Both sides believed that their security – and indeed their survival – was threatened by the dominance of the other. A mini-coup against outgoing President Buyoya by a small faction of military extremists had failed in July 1993. But on 21 October, elements of the Burundian Army launched another coup, this time against President Ndadaye and his government. The President and a number of ministers and leading Hutu – including the entire line of presidential succession – were murdered. A further wave of inter-ethnic killing and pillage followed, resulting in a huge Hutu exodus to Rwanda. The food-crop planting season was missed, causing a 22% fall in agricultural production and the need for substantial food imports.[27] Much damage was also done to private dwellings, and private business and investment left the country. A brave Barundi-led effort to build tolerance and lasting structures had failed.

The Collective Response: International Organisations

As a former Belgian colony within the French sphere of influence, Burundi had impinged little on Western consciousness before 1988. Apart from Belgium, France and the United States, few countries had diplomatic representation in Burundi. The UK, for example, covered both Rwanda and Burundi from Zaire until 1991, and thereafter from Uganda. The assassination of President Ndadaye in 1993 and the scale and level of the subsequent killings and refugee outflows caused outrage in the US and Europe. The US Department of State strongly condemned the overthrow of the elected government as a serious setback to democracy in a country whose democratic success in the June 1993 elections had been an inspiration to the region and to the world. US development aid and military assistance were suspended, and the coup leaders and National Council of Public Safety were held responsible for the safety of all the prisoners they had taken.[28]

Europe followed the US lead. France, in whose embassy the remnants of the Hutu government took refuge, suspended military and economic aid on 23 October (although it did not withdraw its military advisory training team until 1996). Speaking on behalf of Africa, OAU Secretary-General Salim Salim said tellingly that at a time when 'Africa was undergoing the process of democratisation and political renewal, it was unacceptable that the will of the people expressed through the ballot should fall victim to the power of the gun'.[29] Characteristically, Uganda's President Museveni blamed the coup on foreign pressure exerted through the channels that delivered aid, and on external misperceptions of the nature of Barundi society:

> *I was never sure multi-party democracy would work in*
> *Burundi. The ethnic problems in Burundi are well known.*
> *Western nations have a missionary notion of transplanting*
> *their models to Africa.*[30]

At the request of the UN Security Council, Under-Secretary-General for Africa, James Jonah, was sent on an urgent mission to Bujumbura following the military coup attempt. By 27 October, when Jonah arrived, the plot had crumbled. The military high command disowned the plotters and agreed to open the airport to allow Jonah in. From their refuge in the French Embassy, the surviving political leaders – including Prime Minister Sylvie Kinigi – called for international military protection. The atmosphere in the UN, however, after its unsuccessful attempt to deal with the problems in Somalia was not conducive to launching a complex peacekeeping mission with no clear aim. In the light of Jonah's report, the UN Security Council approved the despatch of a small mediation team 'within existing resources' for fact-finding and to facilitate the efforts of the government of Burundi and the OAU to restore calm. UN Secretary-General Boutros-Ghali sent to Bujumbura a senior African official from his own entourage, a former Foreign Minister of Mauritania and a skilled negotiator, Ahmedou Ould Abdallah, to be his Special Representative.

Ould Abdallah arrived on 25 November 1993 to find Bujumbura semi-paralysed by shock. There were estimates of over 50,000 deaths among both the Hutu and the Tutsi, and 375,000 people were said to have fled the country. Ould Abdallah's mandate was fourfold:

- to facilitate contacts between the political parties;
- to restore the legal institutions overthrown on 21 October;
- to conduct an investigation into the coup and the massacres; and
- to cooperate with the OAU (who launched a mixed military/ civilian observer mission in November 1993).

Ould Abdallah's was a feat of containment.[31] From November 1993 to November 1995 he held talks with all the political players with few external tools beyond an understanding of the psychology of the players. He successfully exerted informal pressure on the political class by, for example, indicating knowledge of their overseas bank accounts or by promising visas for overseas visits that did not arrive and scholarships for children that did not materialise. He persuaded local NGO representatives to provide fax machines and newsprint which gave him good access to the media and thus strengthened his hand. He encouraged as many outsiders as possible to pay highly visible official visits, and a regular stream of foreign ministers and senior government officials from the West visited Burundi.

By mid-February 1994, Ould Abdallah had fulfilled the mandate given to him by UN headquarters. Burundi's National Assembly had elected a bureau; the Constitution had been amended to elect the president by indirect ballot; a new Hutu president, Syprien Ntaryamira, had been elected on 13 January 1994 and sworn in on 5 February; and a consensus-based government installed on 11 February. In facilitating and promoting reconciliation, Ould Abdallah had used a newly established group of elders and enlisted the help of foreign representatives to bring pressure to bear. At the request of the elected government, the US lifted its aid embargo against Burundi on 10 December 1993. The Department of State said that it had been encouraged by the Burundian government's efforts to consolidate its control and restore order and democracy to the country. But Washington continued to urge Burundians to cease all violence, respect the authority of the elected government and return to the path of democracy. On the night of 6 April 1994, however, a plane carrying President Habyarimana of Rwanda and President Ntaryamira of Burundi was shot down, triggering the Hutu genocide against the Tutsi in Rwanda. Once news of the two deaths reached him, Ould Abdallah worked through the night. He used his skills as a mediator to mobilise the political élite, and through them the military commanders and provincial governors to discourage any violent reaction. Bujumbura was tense, but it did not ignite. While the violence continued in Rwanda between April and June 1994, in Burundi it was successfully contained.

As the SRSG and sole negotiator, Ould Abdallah had clear authority. By September, the talks with the registered parties had led to a formal agreement on the Convention of Government, which established a basis for power-sharing between the Tutsi and Hutu in the institutions of government. As the agreement noted, trust between the various ethnic groups that make up Burundi's population, and in turn between the people and the institutions, had been profoundly undermined. The aim was for the registered political parties to agree to establish institutions based on 'consensus', on restoring peace, security and trust, and on a state based on the rule of law.[32] Building on Buyoya's earlier initiative, there was to be a national debate within six months on all the basic problems facing the country, to include all elements of Barundi society. Those implicated in the events related to the October 1993 military coup, deliberately described as genocide, were excluded from office at all levels of government. The security services were charged with disarming the civilian population and discouraging violence. They retained their organisational structure, subject to coordination by a future government body. Besides UPRONA and FRODEBU, a long list of political parties signed the Convention, but extremist groups were not represented.

The Convention of Government ultimately proved to be a dead end. It provided a convenient focus for the support of the international community, as did the August 1993 Arusha agreement negotiated between the RPF and the government of Rwanda. Some

Western diplomats believed that the creation of the National Council for the Defence of Democracy (CNDD) and its military wing, the Front for the Defence of Democracy (FDD), and the eventual descent from violence into civil war after 1994, were a direct consequence of the suspension of the Constitution under the Convention.[33] Ould Abdallah conducted the 'best fire-fighting exercise imaginable', as one mediator said, but he was not able to take his mandate beyond firefighting, because he had made the entire Burundian élite dependent on him.[34]

the Convention of Government proved to be a dead end

Ould Abdallah himself believed the Convention was the best deal achievable under the circumstances.[35] The influence of his UN successor was marginal, and it was only with the appointment in 1996 of Mohammed Sahnoun as mediator for the African Great Lakes that the UN re-entered the political game in Burundi.

The UN community had attempted, if not very seriously, to broaden its reach beyond Burundi's political institutions. There was a remarkable coincidence of views between the report of the Security Council mission to Burundi in February 1995 and the very comprehensive report of Special Rapporteur for Human Rights Sergio Pinheiro in October 1995. Pinheiro had found a state of smouldering civil war and an increasingly marked 'genocidal trend of a socio-ethnic nature'.[36] Both reports underlined the dangers of the culture of impunity and emphasised the importance of building an effective judicial system. Other key recommendations included establishing a national police force – acceptable to both parties – and an administrative presence in the provinces, as well as deploying human-rights observers throughout the country. Pinheiro also favoured giving financial support for an independent press, the silencing of 'hate radio' and financial help to integrate the Hutu into the administration. Yet despite these reports, from early 1996 Boutros-Ghali appeared to have lost confidence in the political route. Instead, he became the driving force behind a series of UN proposals for contingency military planning to prevent genocide, and his views became increasingly alarmist.[37] The Security Council was extremely reticent about proposals for military intervention. In the prevailing atmosphere of insecurity, it was difficult to evoke support and funding for human-rights monitoring and such peace-building activities as reforming the judicial system. Nothing happened and an opportunity was lost.

An attempt was, however, made to reduce the problem of impunity. The UN Commission of Enquiry into the murder of President Ndadaye was set up in 1995, and the intrusive nature of its mandate presented problems. Members of the Commission faced closed ranks and a pattern of non-cooperation. Despite the rumours emanating from Bujumbura that the Commission's report, eventually published in August 1996, would indict Buyoya as a key player in the 1993 coup and that the delay in publication was linked to the military coup that he staged in July 1996, the report named no arch plotters. It confirmed again the state of insecurity in all the communes under investigation, and the systematic attacks by the Hutu on the Tutsi in the countryside in response to Ndadaye's murder. Like all other commentators, the writers of the report recognised that impunity was a fundamental problem that could only be suppressed if a fair and effective system of justice were established. And justice could not be administered in the present environment of insecurity.

The UN had become the chosen focus of the Burundian government for international action in 1993, which also suited the major powers. France and Belgium were suspect in Tutsi eyes, France because of its past support for the genocidal regime in Rwanda, and Belgium for the legacy of the colonial period. Neither country showed any wish to take a lead or launch initiatives. France retained its military assistance programme, in the hope that it would exercise some degree of restraint, until 1996, when the Ministry of Cooperation withdrew its remaining trainers, having concluded that their impact was minimal and the locals beyond reason. The UK had no direct concerns in Burundi, but took an informed interest as a permanent member of the Security Council, and a UK diplomatic representative took up residence in Bujumbura in 1996. The European Union took a declaratory stand: it in turn condemned and encouraged, and sent ministerial troikas on visits. In 1995, the EU agreed a 'common position' on Burundi.[38] There was good language on assistance to restore the rule of law, monitor human rights and set up a group of donors. The impact, internationally or on the ground, however, was negligible.

In 1996, the former UN SRSG in Mozambique, Aldo Aiello, was appointed EU Special Envoy to Burundi. The EU also provided some money for the OAU observer mission and promised more for the human-rights observers, if and when they were deployed. This demonstrated the EU's willingness to help with economic and social rehabilitation, once the situation permitted.[39] While funding was always forthcoming for humanitarian emergencies, no European money was given for more innovative peacebuilding, although individual states such as Sweden, Norway and the UK funded imaginative NGO projects to support civil society and promote reconciliation.

The United States followed developments closely through two US special negotiators, one for Burundi and one for the sub-region. Burundi was permanently on its list of states to monitor and also high on its human-rights-abuse list. Washington took the lead in suspending aid following the coups in 1993 and 1996, but it also supported training projects that took Burundian leaders back to the US – indeed, Buyoya himself was a favoured graduate of a programme on democratic leadership.

The Collective Response: The Sub-regional Role

Early in 1997, OAU Secretary-General Salim recalled that despite the many initiatives by African leaders there had been no significant progress towards peace in eastern Zaire. The remark applied equally to the entire African Great Lakes region. Africans, even more than the UN, had been shamed by their inability to respond effectively to genocide in Rwanda. But then, in the mid-1990s, a subtle transformation took place. Africans at the sub-regional level began to take more responsibility for their own futures. Obeisance was paid to outside international efforts, but as UN negotiators proliferated in Burundi and Zaire, key African players began to come forward. President Museveni of Uganda, Vice-President Kagame of Rwanda and Prime Minister Meles Zenawi of Ethiopia constituted one axis, whose agenda became apparent during the course of the rebellion in eastern Zaire in 1996–97.[40] Former President Julius Nyerere of Tanzania, not a member of the 'inner sanctum', was nonetheless regarded as essential because of his status as an elder statesman and his ability to convince and persuade.

In 1994 and 1995, UN and OAU efforts were made in parallel, supported above all by telephone communications between the Secretaries-General. Although these links worked well at the highest level, they were less effective at lower levels. While the UN had Special Representatives on the ground in Rwanda and Burundi and the OAU had a 46-strong military observer mission, it was more difficult to accommodate additional players. In October 1995 on the initiative of former US President Jimmy Carter, the Presidents of Zaire, Uganda and Tanzania – with the concurrence of the Presidents of Burundi and Rwanda – launched a mission to seek agreement on common problems. All the countries of the sub-region harboured a large number of refugees from both Rwanda and Burundi, which was not only an economic burden, but increasingly becoming a political poison. Radical elements were using the camps to plot revenge and invasion, and to secure arms. Carter and Nyerere, together with South Africa's Archbishop Desmond Tutu, were invited to act as co-facilitators for Burundi, and were later joined by the francophone former President of Mali General Amani Toumani Toure. The Carter Centre in Atlanta, Georgia, working with the OAU, organised a summit of African heads of state in Cairo in late November 1995.

This initiative had both its supporters and its detractors. African culture remains highly responsive to 'elder statesmen', and some experts believed the initial mix of negotiators presented a useful balance.[41] The Cairo Declaration, a high point in this innovative – if short-lived – process, was less important for what it achieved than for setting out the views of the African leaders as to the causes of the conflict. The Declaration condemned what it called 'ethnic and political genocide ideology used in the quest for power', and recognised that the security of individuals was a fundamental problem in Burundi. It identified the malevolent activities of those in the Zairean refugee camps; arms supplies and military training that led to cross-border attacks; and inflammatory radio broadcasts. The heads of state did not, however, call for an end to the culture of impunity, although they supported the international tribunal and asked for help in improving Burundi's justice system.[42]

A conference held in Tunis in March 1996 elaborated the commitments to be undertaken at a regional level as well as by Rwanda and Burundi. The Burundian delegation welcomed

Nyerere's role, emphasised the importance of relaunching the national debate and reinvigorating the judicial process, and agreed to start a comprehensive training programme to enhance discipline and professionalism in the security forces. They also agreed to redefine the respective structures and mission of the security and defence forces so that they would assume responsibility for the unity of all elements of the population. Nyerere held a series of follow-up meetings in Mwanza, Tanzania, with representatives of both FRODEBU and UPRONA, and behind the scenes with the extremist leaders. But any progress was made on paper only; the commitments were already divorced from reality.

By now, political dialogue in Burundi had frozen and random killing had become organised insurgency and counter-insurgency. The army stepped up active campaigning against armed groups. Zaire was accused of harbouring Hutu rebels and condoning their raids into Burundi; and indeed the armed wing of the CNDD – the FDD – had its headquarters in Uvira on the other side of Lake Kivu. The government faced increasing reports of massacres of civilians by army units. By summer 1996, the Tutsi, feeling under pressure, began to claim that Nyerere was following a pro-Hutu line. At a regional summit on 24 June at Arusha, President Ntibantunganya gave a graphic account of the inroads made by insurgents in Burundi, and the African leaders agreed to give Burundi security assistance. By the time of the military coup against Ntibantunganya's government on 24 July 1996, the Burundian Army wanted firm action against the FDD, the government had reached stasis and the President and Tutsi Prime Minister Antoine Nduwayo were no longer on speaking terms. The coup was precipitated by a breakaway wing of the army and was directly targeted at the President. When he fled, he left a power vacuum.

The July coup brought the Mwanza process to a halt and provoked the most direct attempt since 1989 by African heads of state to pressure Burundi's leadership. The central organ of the OAU conflict-resolution mechanism (CRM) – a standing council of 15 based at OAU headquarters – met urgently at ambassadorial level in Addis Ababa on 25 July. They made clear that any attempt to assume power by illegal means would not be accepted by the rest of Africa, and that any regime seeking to take over Burundi by force would be isolated and face sanctions. Tanzania called a regional summit at

Arusha on 31 July and, after five hours of discussion, decided to impose economic sanctions as a means of exerting maximum pressure on the new regime in Bujumbura to promote a return to normality. Buyoya was required to restore the National Assembly, reinstate political parties and begin immediate and unconditional negotiations with all parties to the conflict both inside and outside the country. Although the Africans made clear that they did not wish to seek Chapter VII sanctions, the option was left open. In late August, the UN Security Council condemned the coup and supported the efforts of the African leaders.[43]

This was the first time that a group of African countries, with political cover from the OAU-CRM, had taken coercive action against one of their own number, on their own initiative, on a matter that had traditionally been regarded as the 'internal affairs' of another state. The Africans kept to their resolve, closing borders and suspending trade, demonstrating that they were even less willing than in 1993 to accept military-sponsored coups. Tanzania's fingerprints on the agreement were fairly clear. Nyerere's influence over the OAU and his own government was not in question, but his efforts in Burundi had made no significant progress and the disappearance of his fellow facilitators, Carter and Toure, had affected his standing as a negotiator. Burundi's Tutsi Army regarded him as partial and self-interested. Constant diplomatic rumours that the Tanzanian Army was willing to invade Burundi to pre-empt any further major refugee outflow or to act as 'peacekeepers' did not help the situation.

the first African coercive action against one of their own

The decision to impose sanctions, and an economic blockade to enforce them, was inevitably seen as a further Tanzanian power ploy. Nyerere had been personally incensed by the July coup. Toure, himself an ex-military ruler, believed that the attempt to identify Buyoya – who had the standing to create a moderate centre between Hutu and Tutsi – as the prime culprit was mistaken.[44] As in 1989, when aid flows were halted, Buyoya, who had not engineered the coup and had taken office only reluctantly, was under international pressure and donors again suspended aid. The OAU mission, which had laboured since 1993, was withdrawn because of the difficulty of sustaining it under sanctions. The difference between 1996 and 1989 was that Buyoya's room for manoeuvre was now more limited. Polarisation and insecurity were infinitely worse, even than three years earlier.

African voices were much louder in condemning the coup than those of the United States or Europe. Buyoya had Hutu family connections, his earlier reforms had led in 1993 to a democratically elected government, and he had accepted defeat at the polls. He had also taken partial steps towards lifting the ban on parties and allowing the National Assembly to meet, in however inchoate a form. If anyone could bring a degree of coherence to attempts at reconciliation, he could. Yet he was handicapped by his inability to demonstrate that his efforts at home were recognised abroad, and by the fact that the rural population continued to suffer. International opinion was split between those prepared to give him a chance, and those who believed only firmness would pay. In the meantime, while both Buyoya and the rebel Hutu under Leonard Nyangoma had indicated their willingness to enter into negotiations to end hostilities (although only with those not contaminated by the events of 1993), contradictory statements on all sides suggested there was no genuine will to carry these forward in the immediate short term. By the beginning of 1997, sanctions, although still in place, were being evaded and Tutsi entrepreneurs were in control of, and profiting from, fuel deliveries.

The September 1994 Convention of Government represented the high point in negotiations between 1993 and 1996 and provided a focus both domestically and externally. As in the case of the August 1993 Arusha accord for Rwanda, there were constant calls by the international community to carry through the agreement. While conceived as a power-sharing system, it attempted to include some elements of consociation by emphasising consensus and a more inclusive ruling majority, although some critics thought the balance tipped too far in favour of Tutsi interests. But from late 1995 onwards, politics in Burundi, far from making any progress, actually went into reverse. Ould Abdallah left and his successor, a Western diplomat, could not establish the same intellectual and psychological dominance. In Tutsi-dominated Bujumbura, he was presented as playing to a partial, pro-Hutu agenda. Special envoys and negotiators began to proliferate, among them a team assembled by former US President Carter, two US negotiators, an EU envoy and a Belgian. The 'Stedman thesis' applied:

> *Unilateral initiatives by individuals or states acting in competition with the negotiator can prove disastrous to creating the conditions necessary for settlement.*[45]

Ould Abdallah acerbically commented that, before addressing the problems of Burundi, it would be helpful if all the delegates, ambassadors and special envoys present could adopt a common position.[46] Nyerere had been sidelined for being, in Tutsi eyes, pro-Hutu. To the international community, Burundi appeared too complex and intractable. Calls for all Burundians to renounce violence 'and to move single-mindedly along the road to a peaceful and negotiated solution of their problems', or for a return to democracy and the Convention of Government, for the restoration of the 1993 Constitution and for a cease-fire, were more and more beside the point.[47]

The security scene had changed. The Hutu and Tutsi had re-emerged with their old enmities intact. Hutu militia conducted guerrilla attacks in the countryside, in particular in the northern provinces, around Gitega, and in the north-west. When the Burundian Army conducted a successful mission in the north-west against the Hutu armed wing, the FDD, they found highly advanced and modern arms, including shoulder-launched missiles. The FDD headquarters, based in Uvira in eastern Zaire since 1994, was driven out by the rebel Rwandan-speaking Banyamulenge and their allies in late 1996, but re-established in Tanzania, creating a new area of insecurity in eastern Burundi.

Hutu FDD operations were becoming more militarily sophisticated all the time. For their part, the Tutsi Army recruited up to 7,000 new members, largely from the youth militias, to bring their (almost exclusively Tutsi) numbers up to 30,000, and there were rumours that a Burundian invasion of Tanzania was in the offing. Ethnic confrontation had come to penetrate every level of society, not just the political class. Tutsi were largely living in the capital, in provincial capitals and in camps for the displaced in the countryside. Hutu remained mainly in the countryside and were frightened to visit the towns. The Burundian Army created camps for the rural Hutu population 'for their own protection', and in the provinces north of Bujumbura – Cibitoke, Bujumbura Rural and Bubanza – anyone outside the camps was said to be treated as an enemy by both army and rebels. The CNDD/FDD were setting up a parallel administration, FRODEBU was factionalised and there were inevitable divisions and misunderstandings between its leaders in exile and those who remained.[48] Buyoya pursued a gradualist approach with a 'peace plan' that sought to stabilise the internal security situation and hold in parallel an inclusive national debate, to be followed by 'peace conferences' in which all Burundians would participate. At the same time, he continued to lobby for the economic blockade to be lifted on humanitarian grounds. There appeared to be little prospect of political progress.

Track-Two Action: The NGO Contribution

Behind-the-scenes track-two diplomacy by NGOs created some movement between March and May 1997. During the period 1993–95, some international NGO specialists in mediation and conflict management had played a low-key role in Burundi. For the most part, they stayed in touch with the UN SRSG and operated with his full support. They focused on training civil society, backing independent and reliable media, and taking youth and political leaders away from the heated atmosphere for training in, and exposure to, successful examples of reconciliation. A UK-based NGO, International Alert, specialists in conflict management, pursued some imaginative and successful policies in 1994 and 1995. In addition, a training venture, developed with South African and other donor help to train Tutsi and Hutu youth in reconciliation, was successful. A visit by political leaders from Bujumbura to South Africa, culminating in a lecture on reconciliation given by President Nelson Mandela, also had a positive impact.[49]

By 1994–95, however, Barundi civil society had been shattered. Young people and politicians worked well together away from the country, but when they returned home they lacked support structures, and the benefits of their reconciliation training failed to last. Some observers argued that International Alert gave up too soon. They did resume their efforts in 1997, partly in partnership with Search for Common Ground, a Washington-based NGO, which had been working in Bujumbura from 1995 with a team of Hutu and Tutsi journalists to produce 15 hours of radio broadcasting a week to counter 'hate radio'. Search for Common Ground also established a cross-ethnic women's centre. At the same time, an experienced South African mediator worked behind the scenes with moderate elements in the political class to establish some middle ground, and San Egidio, a secretive Catholic lay movement in Rome, which had facilitated the peace process in Mozambique, was active in Burundi through local church organisations from 1995.[50]

Such contributions can be positive or negative; much depends on the personalities involved. For example, a negotiator on behalf of a specialist NGO in West Africa was seen as actively unhelpful and at odds with the UN SRSG and key donors. The work of the same organisation in Burundi, however, was well regarded. The South African negotiator for Search for Common Ground in Bujumbura was experienced, trustworthy and made a real contribution to building political bridges. Search for Common Ground was also imaginative in targeting women, who in Africa play a major role in giving or withholding social approval. Graca Machel has argued passionately for the need to restore the sacredness of women and children in society in African culture. In an admirable experiment, the International Committee of the Red Cross (ICRC) in Mali provided training for a women's group in the basic principles of international humanitarian law. A similar training programme in Burundi could contribute to the development of civil society.[51] Ultimately, a strong civil society would help to deflect impulses to violence, promote understanding of the consequences of ethnic mobilisation and undiluted militant propaganda, and achieve a measure of social stability.

mediation: much depends on personalities

On 16 May 1997, Father Matteo Zuppi, a mediator for San Egidio, confirmed that behind-the-scenes talks between 'the government in place in Burundi' and the CNDD, involving Nyangoma, had reached agreement on a seven-point route to a comprehensive settlement.[52] The negotiating agenda covered:

• the restoration of Constitutional and institutional order;
• issues relating to the armed forces and police;

- a suspension of hostilities;
- justice, including setting up an international criminal tribunal;
- involvement of other parties in the political process;
- a cease-fire; and
- guarantees on the means of carrying through an overall agreement.

Once again, the talks had been backed financially by the government of Norway, whose Foreign Ministry had the unique ability to provide swift and discreet funding to track-two mediation efforts, as it had done for the Middle East peace process. San Egidio was able to profit from FRODEBU's change of approach, entailing a recognition that the outside world would not impose Hutu rule on Burundi, whether by sanction or intervention. On the other side, in Bujumbura, UPRONA did not react as adversely as might have been expected to direct contacts with Nyangoma. Buyoya publicly confirmed the talks with CNDD on 30 May as 'preparatory talks for the great negotiations that will start soon in the region and will bring together all Burundian political protagonists', and also allow regional countries to make a contribution. Even for the Tutsi, Nyerere remained in play.[53]

The Impact of Collective Action

The history of Burundi during the period 1993–97 was a tragedy in several acts. The political leaders pulled down their own house over themselves, set fire to the timbers and laid waste the land. The degree of ethnic mobilisation was catastrophic and will take generations to reverse. While the Barundi showed no disposition to sort out their problems for themselves, the collective international response also proved incoherent and fitful. The conflicts of Burundi proved unresponsive to political pressure, whether from the UN Security Council, from the OAU or from military threat.

political leaders pulled down their own house

Written declarations were worth no more than the paper on which they appeared. According to Sahnoun, 'the incoherence of effort of the international community allowed the parties to the conflict to do what they wished since they could always find someone to back them'.[54] The use of ethnicity as a deliberate political tool, the crucial interplay between Rwanda and Burundi and, from 1994, the role of refugee camps in eastern Zaire as a breeding ground for revanchism came late to policy-makers, as did the absolute determination of demographic minority regimes in Rwanda and Burundi to continue to hold power in the interests of 'self-preservation'.

By the end of May 1997, while Western eyes were distracted by developments in Zaire, a process was in train in Burundi involving many strands which had the potential to be mutually reinforcing. The elements traditionally identified for ending civil wars – a mutually damaging stalemate and a reduction of the asymmetry of the local parties' organisation and status – were beginning to come into focus.[55] Members of the Barundi political class began to engage with track-two players on the domestic agenda. Search for Common Ground concentrated on building trust and relationships between key players in UPRONA and FRODEBU, while San Egidio focused on the elements that could lead to a suspension of hostilities. Externally, it was universally recognised that an easy transition to a new regime in Kinshasa could contribute to stability in the sub-region as a whole, not least if it increased security along the borders. Nyerere had always argued that the problems of the sub-region had to be taken as a single entity. Whatever the weaknesses of the colonial legacy, there was no obvious pressure for border changes. Africa and the West were publicly and legally committed within the framework of the OAU and the OSCE to the sanctity of existing borders; adjustments to 'living space' were not possible.

Some political analysts have argued that the rhetoric of mobilisation in ethnic conflict so hardens attitudes that cross-ethnic appeals have no impact, and that a stable settlement is possible only by separating warring groups and establishing a balance of relative strength that makes it unprofitable for either party to overturn the settlement.[56] So far, this analysis has not received support. Future stability requires four elements:

- a viable 'experiment in home-grown democracy', in the words of Jan van Eck, which could give Hutu and Tutsi alike a share in the state;[57]

- a considerable investment in civil society to start reversing the use of ethnicity as the principal source of identity;
- a serious attempt to promote accountability for acts of violence and an end to the culture of impunity; and
- a sub-regional settlement.

Some of the fertile land of eastern Zaire might provide not so much a buffer zone (seen to be the first aim of the 1996 Kivu rebellion), but an oxygen lung for some of the people of Rwanda and Burundi by providing an additional area within which they could move, work and farm, without requiring any formal change in borders. Any such possibility would raise intense political difficulties and could work only as part of an overall package for peace that brought together politics, security, development, justice and human rights for the sub-region – once a new regime has settled down in Kinshasa. Active and fast support for a comprehensive, if small-scale, process for the sub-region along the lines of the 1947 Marshall Plan for Europe and under the auspices of the UN family – from the UN Development Programme (UNDP) to the UNHCR and the World Bank – which allowed some freedom of movement to less densely populated areas, could transform the sub-region. International representatives were developing such concepts in March 1997.[58]

While preventive diplomacy is always the preferred course of action, there
are some situations when it must be backed by a credible threat to use force
in order to stave off humanitarian disaster.
Former UN Secretary-General Boutros Boutros-Ghali, 1996

I have never believed that foreign troops could restore peace.
Foreign Minister of Burundi Venerand Bakevyumusaya, 5 July 1996

chapter 2

External Military Intervention
Versus Local Action

Violent social conflict within a state is rarely confined within its own
borders. Thus the problems of Burundi and Rwanda became locked
into the broader question of sub-regional stability. By late 1996, the
African Great Lakes region was in crisis. By mid-1997, the scenario
affecting the sub-region, even if not a formal settlement, was beginning to emerge. The simplistic Western agenda of well-ordered peace
talks based on a cease-fire, with military intervention considered
only for humanitarian purposes, was overtaken by a fast-moving
African-dictated agenda, using both violence and psychology.

   In late 1996, minority Tutsi governments in both Burundi and
Rwanda disenfranchising Hutu majorities, attrition by killing
between ethnic communities in Burundi, the arming and training of
militant Hutu in exile or in refugee camps – determined to fight their
way back into Rwanda and indeed Burundi – created an explosive
mix. Zairean politicians, resentful of the success and discipline of the
Rwandan-speaking Banyamulenge, who had settled in Kivu
province during successive waves of immigration dating as far back
as the eighteenth century, further inflamed the situation by
excluding them from citizenship on the basis of the 1981 Zairean
Nationality Act.[1] Using regionalism or ethnicity to buy off popular
protest had long been a tool of the Mobutu regime. The increased
violence that flowed from active discrimination against those of
Tutsi origin had been well noted and prepared for. As the Bishop of
Goma, Monsignor Faustin Ngabu, had noted: 'the authorities, which

should be coming to the aid of the victims of violence, seem on the contrary to wish to feed the flames'.[2] Zaireans close to Mobutu had also been complicit in allowing, and indeed organising, a steady flow of arms to the ex-armed forces of Rwanda (FAR), the *Interahamwe* Hutu militia in the refugee camps, and to the exiled Burundian Hutu rebels headquartered in Uvira, across Lake Tanganyika from Bujumbura. The Banyamulenge rebellion began in direct response to the one-week deadline for the 'immigrants' to leave, announced by the governor of South Kivu in September 1996. Fuelled by close links with, and unacknowledged support from, the governments of Rwanda, Uganda and even Burundi, the dramatic success of the rebels brought into salience the phantom nature of the state of Zaire in the east.

When Zairean and Rwandan forces exchanged mortar fire across the border at Cyangugu on 31 October 1996, the conflict took on an international dimension. By 4 November, Goma had fallen. By mid-November, the rebel forces under Laurent Kabila had conducted a spectacular rout of the Zairean Army and attacked the Hutu militia dominating the refugee camps around Goma. Two years of angst in the international community was resolved when some 700,000 Rwandan refugees, liberated from *Interahamwe* dominion, streamed back across the border to Rwanda. The problems of Rwanda and Burundi became overshadowed by the perceived threat posed to the stability of Zaire and the Mobutu regime by the wider agenda of the rebel leader, an anti-Mobutu veteran of the 1960s civil war. By March 1997, the press carried reports of a US-inspired plot to partition Zaire in order to provide a greater living area for the Rwandan Hutu.[3] By May, even France had recognised that the Mobutu regime was finished and French commentators lamented the loss of a major zone of interest. The initial exclusion of a French (as indeed of any European) representative from the US–South African–UN peace talks held on a South African naval vessel on 4 May was balanced by the US negotiator, Permanent Representative to the UN Bill Richardson, who described the US and France as 'catalysts' in the process to a post-Mobutu regime and as 'working towards the same solution'.[4]

Between 1993 and 1996, problems of security in the region had developed three clear facets:

Map 2 *Rwanda and Burundi*

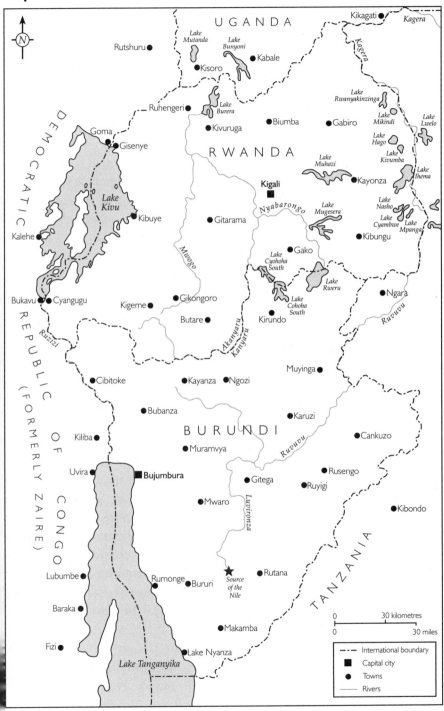

- relations based on fear between the Hutu and Tutsi communities within Rwanda and Burundi;
- political spillage from their violent domestic disputes to neighbouring countries, particularly Zaire; and
- long-standing Western concern about the strategic implications of the possible collapse of Zaire and the Mobutu regime.

The Kivu rebellion in 1996 – centred on Tutsi links versus an impotent Zairean state allied with the Hutu militias – demonstrated clear local determination to solve some of the security problems, given the lack of decisive action by the West. Moreover, the emergence of a new Anglophone axis of strong leaders, including Ugandan President Museveni, Rwandan Vice-President Kagame, Ethiopian Prime Minister Meles and John Garang of the Sudan People's Liberation Front (SPLF) – all widely believed to have the sympathy, if not the direct support, of the Anglo-Saxon world in a traditionally Francophone area – generated tension.[5]

Rwanda apart, between 1993 and 1997 proposals for external military intervention were of three types:

- to protect individuals or groups;
- preventive deployment and security assistance; and
- humanitarian intervention to save lives.

In October 1993, Burundi's deposed government asked for international protection; the UN Secretary-General argued for a preventive deployment and rapid-response capability to cope with a potential crisis in the country at intervals between December 1994 and early 1996; African leaders supported military intervention or security assistance in 1996; and there was considerable pressure for intervention with the conflicting aims of avoiding a humanitarian crisis and/or restoring the rule of law in eastern Zaire in late 1996, and sporadically to help with refugees until the definitive end of the Mobutu regime in May 1997.

Africa's leaders, and indeed the UN until the departure of SRSG Ould Abdallah in November 1995, saw the implications for sub-regional stability much earlier than the West. Leaders met at

OAU summits, within the ambit of the new conflict-resolution mechanism and, most to the point, among leaders of the states of the African Great Lakes. Former President Nyerere regretted the lack of results; but that is not to discount the efforts made or the progressive evolution of embryonic tools for dealing with conflict within the OAU and at the sub-regional level. The Africans' preference for political action in the first instance reflected their lack of logistic and financial capability for military intervention, together with their long-standing collective inhibition about interfering in the domestic affairs of their own brotherhood. In their quest for a political solution, the African leaders preferred traditional skills and talking through problems under the guidance of a respected statesman or elders. In the words of General Toure of Mali, a military commander and ex-president who had himself seized power and then organised elections to bring back civilian rule: 'wherever troops have been sent, especially in Africa, they have not solved any problems. The solutions lay in the hearts of people and not guns'.[6]

The West had yet to adjust its conflict-management techniques from those of the Cold War in which pressure on acknowledged leaders at the governmental level could pay dividends. The conflicts of the African Great Lakes were not ideological insurgencies, but brutal power struggles, and the pressures were not those of East–West confrontation, but of ending abuse and saving lives. The key players were often at the sub-state level and not easily amenable to 'positive and negative inducement'.[7] Western pressure groups, urged on by the powerful NGO community that had occupied

> *the conflicts were not ideological insurgencies, but brutal power struggles*

Kigali and Goma from mid-1994, generated regular, well-publicised appeals for military intervention on humanitarian grounds. Soundbites or headlines such as 'Burundi Blood-bath Runs its Course as West Looks On', in 1993, and 'Oxfam Warns Burundi Faces Blood-bath Without Aid', in 1996, became common. Later in 1996 the tone intensified. 'How many lives have to be in danger, how many people missing to justify a deployment of troops by the civilised world?' were the emotive words of EU Commissioner for Humanitarian Affairs Emma Bonino, while French Foreign Minister

Hervé de Charette warned that 'there are the makings of the greatest tragedy in human history' if the West failed to intervene in eastern Zaire.[8]

Guilt about the events in Rwanda, and lack of familiarity with the complexities of the area and with the characteristics of such conflicts led to a series of ill-conceived and impracticable proposals born of desperation, which died as the publicity surrounding them died. In media terms, as the crisis in eastern Zaire supervened, so the crisis in Burundi disappeared. Whereas Burundi was a dangerous, difficult and complex country, Zaire had natural resources, and a rebellion in the eastern part of the country was accessible (at least initially), comprehensible and a potentially rich source of human-interest stories and pictures. The oddity lay in the disjunction between the proposals for intervention and the political attempts to manage and contain successive crises. As one experienced NGO observer acutely commented:

> With the end of the Cold War, aid has become a substitute for foreign policy, which is both expensive and very dangerous. Aid agencies have become the new front line because no one else is interested.[9]

In fact none of the various proposals, from appeals to protect government figures to intervention to inhibit genocide, led to an actual deployment.

As of March 1997, the only authorised foreign military personnel in Burundi or Zaire were 46 unarmed OAU military observers who served from 1993 to 1996, and a small headquarters briefly set up in Entebbe for the abortive MNF in late 1996.[10] As in the 1960s, Zaire did attract a number of adventurers, mercenaries and 'advisers'. Angola's *União Nacional para a Independência Total de Angola* (UNITA) had old links with Mobutu, and there were reports that the Mozambique government had given help to the rebels. There was also some involvement of trained Tutsi: whether these were Banyamulenge from eastern Zaire who had taken part in the RPF campaign or Rwandans was kept deliberately hidden until the fall of Kinshasa, when English- and Swahili-speaking troops wearing the Wellington boots favoured by the RPF were visibly deployed in the city.[11]

Proposals for Protection

Brian Urquhart, the father of UN peacekeeping, said in 1991 that it was impossible to place a UN blue-helmeted doorman in every ethnically mixed apartment building in Bosnia. Echoing him, Ould Abdallah said that 'it is not possible to put a blue helmet behind every Burundian'.[12] In Burundi, from 1993 onwards, the Hutu wish for external military intervention was based on the assumption that such a force would counterbalance the Tutsi Army and might even be manipulated into attacking it. On the other side, the Tutsi Army repeatedly made clear that it would meet any external military intervention with force: in Tutsi mythology, foreign troops would favour the Hutu and be antagonistic to the interests of the Tutsi. Experts on the region believed that any military insertion would start a new wave of large-scale massacres. A chain reaction began with the murder of President Ndadaye on 21 October 1993, at the moment when he had been planning to replace 2,000–2,500 Tutsi in the Burundian Army with Hutu elements drawn from the extremist wing of FRODEBU. As in Rwanda in 1993–94, proposals to change the ethnic balance in the armed forces triggered extreme violence.[13]

The murder of Burundi's first elected President by elements of the military launched an orgy of violence, the like of which had not been seen since 1972. The Hutu reacted against the Tutsi in a bloody 'collective rage'. The Tutsi, in turn, reacted violently against the Hutu and there were savage reprisals by the army.[14] By 25 October, an estimated 50,000 Hutu had been killed, 300,000 left the country, and large numbers of both groups were internally displaced. Six days after Ndadaye's murder, when the military coup was already being disowned by the military leadership, Tutsi Prime Minister Kinigi appealed from her refuge in the French Embassy for a foreign force to help restore Burundi's legitimate institutions. Asked if she had in mind the UN or the OAU, Prime Minister Kinigi was indifferent: 'anyone who might respond to our appeal'.[15]

The military command opened Bujumbura airport to let UN Under-Secretary-General Jonah land on 27 October. The next day, thousands of Hutu marched in Bujumbura to support international military intervention to end the prodigious violence. A Hutu activist from the late President's party told reporters:

If we do not get an international military force, blood will continue to flow. The government cannot come out [of hiding] because we are sure the army is waiting to slaughter them as they did the President.[16]

The same day, Kinigi asked Jonah for 1,000 foreign troops to protect members of the government, to help disband and reform the army, and to guard strategic installations and buildings. Her appeal clearly found some echo, despite a restrictive mandate from New York and the Secretary-General's reluctance to take on any complex new missions in the aftermath of the Somalia debacle.[17] Jonah announced on 29 October that the military were back in their barracks and that the UN might send 100 peacekeepers to protect government leaders. He suggested that the UN might issue a contract to a private security company rather than use military personnel.[18] Kinigi, still clinging to the idea of an intervention force, stated publicly on 31 October that the UN would provide a security force to protect government ministers, key officials and strategic installations. Both statements were promptly disavowed in New York by the Secretary-General's spokesman, who stressed that peacekeeping missions needed Security Council authorisation and no such resolution had been adopted. Once back in New York, away from Bujumbura and under a different kind of pressure from the US government – who had made plain its intention to oppose any UN peacekeeping mission in Burundi – Jonah retreated.

After the ignominy of the UN intervention in Somalia, the combination of an African state, an internal conflict and a request to protect local government figures had no appeal in New York. Instead, the ball bounced back to the Africans. At a regional summit in Kigali on 29 October, the Presidents of Rwanda, Tanzania and Zaire issued a communiqué calling urgently for a military force to help end the tribal killings in the Burundian countryside and restore trust and security to the country as a whole. Africans, they said, must make a concrete gesture to stop massacres of innocent Burundians and help find a lasting solution to the tribal violence. The Secretaries-General of the OAU and UN should create an international force for stabilisation and to restore trust, made up from African countries and selected in consultation with the legitimate government of Burundi.[19] Museveni promptly offered a Ugandan contingent. Faced with UN reservations, the Burundian government formally asked the OAU for an intervention force of 1,000 on 1 November.

OAU Secretary-General Salim responded with caution. He had secured endorsement of the new conflict-resolution mechanism in July with great difficulty and in the face of considerable reservations from some states about its potential intrusiveness. As a Tanzanian, he understood something of the nature of the problems in Burundi and talks in Bujumbura confirmed his doubts. Money and logistics were also a problem. Speaking on departure from Kigali, he said there were still difficulties in deploying an intervention force. The government wished to be protected by foreign troops, but the army did not want foreign troops in the country.

Prime Minister Kinigi tried to change the army's mind, explaining that the foreign force would not be an intervention or interposition force. Instead, its mission would be to restore confidence and it would cooperate with the national army. Despite Chief of the General Staff Jean Bikomagu's claim to Jonah on 28 October that the army had accepted the government's authority and orders, on 1 November the army rejected out of hand proposals by the surviving members of the government to deploy foreign troops. The army spokesman said:

> *The Burundi army totally rejects any attempts to deploy foreign troops anywhere in the country. This is against our laws, against Burundi's common good ... we [the military] cannot understand what the government means by calling for foreign protection. The Burundi army is capable of securing the lives of its leaders.*[20]

Even civil servants and representatives of political parties opposed the deployment of a foreign force. The opposition to external intervention was to remain a leitmotif for the next three years.[21] The arrival of 15 French *gendarmes* on 5 November to help protect the French Embassy and the former government ministers within it did not help, and was seen as humiliating.

An emissary from the OAU Secretary-General arrived in Bujumbura on 2 November. He accepted the need to take into account the views of both government and army regarding bringing foreign troops into the country and proposed a mixed military–

civilian approach to restore trust and confidence: 200 military observers would be despatched from several African countries – among them some Burundians – supported by a civilian observation mission. Jean-Marie Ngendahayo, Minister for Communications (and later Foreign Affairs) – and, although a member of the traditional *Ganwa* ruling class, increasingly the public face of the former government – believed the force would be too small: 180 military and 20 civilian observers would scarcely protect the government, let alone provincial governors and regional authorities. On 21 November, the military high command held eight hours of discussion with FRODEBU Chairman (later President) Ntibantunganya on the proposal for an international protection force. The army command again argued that deploying such a force would be humiliating, but the government lost patience, stating that it was no longer prepared to be a testing ground for the army's confidence in it. The proposed OAU intervention force of 180 soldiers and 20 civilians agreed on 20 November was scaled down at the insistence of the Burundian Army, and because of the practical difficulties the force posed for OAU members. When the 40-strong mission finally deployed at the end of 1994, it had an equal balance of military and civilians.[22]

The international debate about a potential military intervention in Burundi contained the main elements, and all the confusion, of the debate that would continue in various guises during the next three years. Protecting government leaders and provincial personalities was hardly a task for an impartial peacekeeping force, since it would set the force against a hostile army from the outset. African neighbours paid lip-service to the idea of an external force to promote security, but did not attempt to offer any concept of operations. In the highly charged environment of Burundi, an external force would have changed the local dynamics. Rather than promote security, the mission would have heightened Tutsi insecurity. Short of a powerful Western-led force prepared to confront and disarm all sources of violence, a small and lightly armed force dependent on the consent of all parties would have been held hostage by the army, unable to assert its right to move

an external force would have heightened Tutsi insecurity

freely and to protect the civilian population. Faced with this army hostility, the foreign force would have become too easily aligned with the Hutu cause. Leading Western powers may not have understood the exact nature of the conflict in Burundi, but the difficulties were obvious enough to make them wish to steer clear of the problem. The Africans, for their part, had neither the capability to act nor any clear vision of what foreign troops might actually do.

The initial post-Cold War self-confidence of the international community, characterised, in Boutros-Ghali's telling phrase, by an 'excess of expectation', had reached both a high and a low point in 1993. The expectation of the international community had been that there could be recourse to the UN at any time for military support against aggression, to protect a fragile government or minority or to support a peace settlement. The major UN member-states and military powers would be willing to deploy troops for such purposes in areas far from their own countries and where they had no direct interests at stake. But with major UN operations in place simultaneously in Cambodia, Somalia and the former Yugoslavia, the Department of Peacekeeping Operations (DPKO) was stretched to the limit and criticism of it was mounting from troop-contributing countries. In July 1993, Somali women hacked 24 Pakistani peacekeepers to death, and the following September, Somali militia troops downed a US helicopter, killing the US pilots, whose bodies were dragged through the capital's streets. New US enthusiasm for peacekeeping wilted in the face of public horror. President Clinton told the UN General Assembly in September 1993 that the UN could not solve all the world's problems and must learn to say 'no'. When he received no support in New York for a mission to Burundi the following month, Jonah told the press that the UN was over-stretched and underfunded, and all indications were that the Council did nor want to assume new peacekeeping tasks.[23] 'We are now realising that governments aren't prepared to take casualties except in their own national interest'.[24]

The UN Security Council approved the despatch of a small mediation team under Ould Abdallah for fact-finding and to facilitate the efforts of the OAU and the government of Burundi to restore order. The OAU observers who were finally deployed in November were unarmed and had poor logistical support, but they gained direct operational experience and witnessed developments on the ground. Ould Abdallah believed that the Burundian Army was comfortable with the OAU observer presence. While they relieved some of the external pressures, they could also be easily circumvented and controlled. Until the mission finally left in September 1996 following the imposition of OAU sanctions against Burundi, the observers survived in a maelstrom of killing with no casualties. Nevertheless, the OAU and their observers deserve some credit for this mission, which obviated the promised resistance of the Burundian Army to any external military intervention by force. The small UN mediation mission and the separate team of OAU observers were a striking mix, acceptable precisely because they were unthreatening, and, thanks to the personality of Ould Abdallah, highly effective. SRSG Ould Abdallah never supported a serious military intervention. He knew it would make matters worse, precipitate massacres in the short term and, given Burundi's circumstances, its stay would need to be protracted 'perhaps 50 years, sufficient time to train two generations of Burundians to live together peacefully'.[25]

Preventive Deployment

After the events of 1994 in Rwanda, the fear of another genocide and, even more, of accusations that not enough had been done to prevent it, coloured the proposals and reactions of the UN, the Africans and the West. Somewhat unfairly, Boutros-Ghali already carried the burden of blame for the failure of the UN mission in Somalia. The inability of the small UN peacekeeping force in Rwanda to contain the genocide in 1994, when it lacked capacity and was further hindered by the precipitate departure of Belgian and Bangladeshi units, left scars and had been well noted in Africa. An African himself, and supported by an African Under-Secretary-General for Peacekeeping, Boutros-Ghali not only kept Burundi in focus, but also tirelessly proposed concepts for military intervention from mid-1994.

Boutros-Ghali first enlisted Security Council support on 19 August 1994 in an oral report in which he called for a preventive multinational force in Zaire that could intervene rapidly to prevent genocide if the situation in Burundi deteriorated. He repeated his proposals in October 1994, adding a request for a contingent of guards similar to those in Iraq to protect humanitarian organisation teams, and a third time in December 1995, after Abdallah's resignation.[26] There were, however, already private doubters in the DPKO and the Secretary-General encountered considerable scepticism when he raised it with the five Permanent Members of the Security Council. Boutros-Ghali had moved a long way from his insistence on firm action against Mohamed Farah Aideed in Somalia a year earlier. His proposal in mid-1994 that the five-member Contact Group for Bosnia provide a force to take over responsibility from the UN Protection Force (UNPROFOR) had not been adopted, and he was increasingly looking to NATO to take on these difficult tasks. On the one hand, Boutros-Ghali appeared to wish to establish a good track record for alerting the international community to potential crises, while keeping his own hands clean for possible re-election as Secretary-General the following year.

the UN was overloaded with enforcement missions

On the other hand, the experience of Somalia, Rwanda and increasingly Bosnia suggested that the UN was overloaded with applications for enforcement missions, which were best conducted in a multinational framework by a coalition of the willing and the able. The truth probably lay somewhere between the two.

The proposed preventive mission in Zaire provoked a predictable litany of questions. What was the political objective? What would be the concept of operations? How many troops would be involved? Where would they be based? What about logistics? With what rules of engagement? Who would pay? As the situation in Burundi had been fragile for so long, what would be the trigger for their active involvement? For how long would troops deploy? And when could they be released? The Secretary-General's own report in October 1994 had paid tribute to the contribution made by his representative in Bujumbura towards containing violent reactions in Burundi when the genocide began in Rwanda. For the practitioners of the Security Council, a preventive mission in Zaire risked generating new complications; there was already pressure from NGOs to send a military expedition to root out the militants and killers from the refugee camps and defuse tension between different groups in eastern Zaire. Could a mission be separated from Hutu revanchism, whether within Burundi or by exiles from both countries?

The Secretary-General tried again in February 1996, calling for a stand-by force for humanitarian intervention in Burundi. Personnel, up to a maximum of 25,000, would be trained, earmarked and ready to deploy at short notice as a multinational force under Chapter VII of the UN Charter. If a humanitarian military operation proved necessary, the force's mandate would be to prevent massacres, provide security to refugees, displaced persons and civilians at risk, and protect key economic installations. The force would be deployed to selected areas of actual or potential confrontation. Because the purpose was humanitarian, the force would not engage in combat as long as it was not impeded from carrying out its mandate.[27] This proposal attracted as little enthusiasm as had the Secretary-General's first one, although its objectives were both mixed and wide-ranging. Experience in Bosnia had already shown that effectively protecting the civilian population against attack by local armed elements required a major military commitment. The Secretary-General was calling for an open-ended commitment in an operation of considerable complexity – as any map of Burundi could indicate – and without any clear objective.

Gossip in the UN corridors in New York murmured of 'alibi-building'. Boutros-Ghali's argument that an assertive approach, involving contingency planning for a coalition force, would impact on the Burundian Army was not convincing. UN reports had painted a very clear picture of the current environment in Burundi: of the problems presented by the culture of fear and mutual insecurity; of the proliferation of armed groups; and of fundamental army hostility to any military intervention. The recommendation thus did not seem to follow from the analysis. While the suggestion for a contingency coalition operation fell on deaf ears, there was clear agreement that the UN could not entirely abandon its responsibilities. The Security Council firmly invited the UN Secretary-General to carry out planning for a contingency humanitarian operation in Burundi.[28]

The Africans were faced with the same dilemma. The June 1995 OAU summit at Yaounde determined that, if internal conflict intensified, the response should not exclude a military intervention for humanitarian purposes. When the ball passed back to the UN court there was no resentment, given that the Africans were known to have had structural difficulties in mounting a military operation.

African chiefs of staff in any case were generally in favour of a UN helmet and the associated funding it brought. The high running costs of the Economic Organisation of West African States (ECOWAS) Monitoring Group (ECOMOG) in Liberia had been a painful lesson, even with US support. Former President Nyerere regarded military planning as a useful adjunct to his negotiating efforts. Plans for a positive outcome – with a peacekeeping force – and plans for a negative outcome – implicitly with an enforcement mission – could, he argued, strengthen his hand with the Burundians.

In reality, the concept had the reverse effect. Nyerere's support for military contingency planning came to be seen as a Tanzanian national agenda and affected Tutsi perceptions of his impartiality. At Tanzanian prompting, military planning talks involving officers from Tanzania, Kenya and Uganda took place at Arusha in May and June 1996. At this summit, attended by Burundian President Ntibantunganya and Minister of Defence Lieutenant Colonel Firmin Sinzoyiheba, the Burundian delegation agreed the provision of security assistance as approved by the National Committee for Security. With the concurrence of the Burundian delegation (albeit with less willingness by some, notably Prime Minister Nduwayo), the Arusha summit decided to establish a technical committee headed by Tanzania with experts from Ethiopia, Uganda and Rwanda to examine the modalities of such assistance.[29] The US and the UK offered planning help. At a series of technical meetings, an African plan was developed for a Chapter VI operation under UN and OAU auspices, which envisaged a Tanzanian and a Ugandan area of operations in Burundi, with safe zones for persecuted civilians. Western nations would be invited to foot the bill.

The Burundian Army reacted to the planning process with hostility and refused to welcome the technical committee or to provide the basic information on which the group could work. The Tutsi Prime Minister accused President Ntibantunganya of a sell-out and of seeking to 'neutralise' the army. The Minister of Defence reversed his position and made clear his view that foreign troops could not restore peace. Tutsi extremists used this opportunity to create trouble and launched the student militia onto the streets to demonstrate against the possible deployment of foreign troops and in favour of overthrowing the government and forming a patriotic front to defend Burundian sovereignty. Military coup plans accelerated. In 1993, proposals to reform the army had been one of the key triggers to the murder of President Ndadaye. Three years later, an attempt to provide military assistance, even to support the army, was seen as a direct threat to Tutsi security, and Tanzanian involvement was inflammatory. The coup took place on 25 July. Major Buyoya was not, however, one of the plotters and was reluctant, when approached, to return to government.

In response, and at Tanzanian prompting, the African leaders of the sub-region met again on 31 July at Arusha. A member of the technical committee reported that it had drawn up a plan for military intervention if so instructed by the heads of state: 'it's up to them to decide'.[30] The leaders noted with appreciation the work undertaken by the technical committee, but abandoned plans for military intervention and indeed placed military planning on the back burner. Instead, the summit opted to impose voluntary sanctions, backed in turn by the central organ of the OAU conflict-resolution mechanism.[31]

Difficulties had become apparent at the early stages of planning. The West had made clear that it would not fund the operation, estimated at $2–3bn for a force of 25,000, and had doubts about the way in which it would function with separate Ugandan and Tanzanian areas of operation. Given Ugandan links with the Tutsi and President Museveni's own Hima background, a Ugandan zone would be more than likely to attract Tutsi, while a Tanzanian area would attract Hutu. Huge ethnic camps of displaced persons could be created on a lasting basis, together with a very lengthy military commitment, which Africans could not sustain alone.

Military intervention took second place to economic pressure and Rwanda fell into line over regional sanctions. The OAU observers were withdrawn from Burundi in August because of the difficulties of operating under a sanctions regime, and the UN was invited to continue contingency military planning. Boutros-Ghali told Nyerere in October that he believed the worst could happen at any moment and that he was continuing to encourage states with a logistical capability to stand ready to prevent a repeat of the events in Rwanda. But his latest proposals, whether for a multinational force or for a UN-led operation, had found no welcome. Only five of the 31 states contacted by the Secretariat bothered to reply to invitations to contribute, and four of the five replies were negative. The Secretary-General concluded that there did not yet seem to be sufficient political will for 'resolute preventive action'.[32]

The complexities of Burundian politics, the constant pattern of killing and difficulties in finding a basis for political movement had a strange consequence. The international community, as if in desperation, had elected to discuss military intervention almost as an alibi for political inaction, rather than to reinforce a peace plan. The Secretary-General's proposals and invitation to the Secretariat to undertake contingency planning were 'semaphore flags' of concern without an underlying reality. The approach achieved the worst of all

talk of military intervention as an alibi for political inaction

possible outcomes. After three years of discussion, which had led to the deployment of only 46 OAU observers, the signals were not credible. Yet they provided the Tutsi extremists and armed forces with every excuse to procrastinate and make trouble.

Burundi was a matter for renewed concern from July to October 1996. Then developments in eastern Zaire supplanted Burundi and international interest declined. The situation in Burundi continued to evolve, however. By late 1996, the proliferation of armed bands and random killing had given way in some provinces to better armed and trained Hutu units. Northern provinces were increasingly Hutu militia-controlled and subject to wide-ranging guerrilla attack, while the cities were largely Tutsi-dominated. From random attacks, tactics on both sides had changed. The Buyoya government relocated large concentrations of civilians into camps or 'regrouping centres', allegedly for their own protection and to improve the security situation. The army also pursued 'cordon-and-search' policies. Both Hutu rebels and the security forces targeted civilians outside the camps in the three north-western provinces worst affected by insurgency and, from early 1997, the Hutu militants switched their headquarters to Dar es Salaam following the fall of Uvira to Zairean rebels. With the change in demographic geography, a minority government not fully in control of its own security forces sought to counter an insurgency by extremists in the name of the demographic majority, a position which in the long run was unsustainable, and seen as such by neighbouring states.[33]

Humanitarian Operations

Burundi was supplanted as an issue by Zaire, not because circumstances changed, but because the weight of the humanitarian lobby was brought to bear on a new crisis. The complexity of the issues, political stalemate and genuine dangers for outsiders in Burundi (three ICRC personnel were killed) limited the humanitarian presence, and the media went elsewhere. The horror of the refugee camps in eastern Zaire was well known from the time of the 1994 exodus; so was the fact that the camps held many of the extremists and killers who had participated in the genocide. There was evidence also that the Hutu were well supplied with funds and arms; the British Broadcasting Corporation had shown television footage of military training in the camps. In Rwandan eyes, the Kinshasa government and close relatives of Mobutu were implicated.[34] UNHCR efforts between 1994 and 1996 to gather support for removing armed elements from the camps, to avoid contravening the terms of its own mandate, had been fruitless, and it began to consider withdrawing its assistance from the camps altogether.

On 8 September 1996, the governor of Zaire's South Kivu province provoked a new crisis by giving 200,000 Tutsi Banyamulenge – long resident in the area, but termed 'illegal immigrants' – one week in which to leave the country. The ensuing rebellion began with a core of these Banyamulenge and recruited more from other groups as it progressed. Laurent Kabila, an old Mobutu antagonist, businessman and adventurer, became the rebel front man after the fall of Uvira. The rebel movement used some highly effective psychological tactics, from the initial use of the *Mai Mai* – a mystical militia with some of the attributes of the *Kamajors* in Sierra Leone – to announcing the imminent fall of towns while leaving an exit route open and making a serious attempt to enlist the support of the civilian population. Rwandan uniforms were spotted at Goma, as well as some familiar faces from the 1994 RPF campaign. Regular denials of participation by Ugandan and Rwandan governments were not wholly accepted, and Rwandan spokesmen conceded that they had taken part in a cross-border raid in October from

Cyangugu and that some Banyamulenge had actively supported the RPF campaign in 1994.

It was possible to trace, in earlier campaigns in the sub-region, an intellectual parentage at the very least; Kabila had had links with Museveni in the past, and the effectiveness of his operation recalled the RPF in 1994 under Kagame, who himself admitted privately 'of course, there is a link'.[35] In July 1997, Kagame publicly admitted that the Rwandan government planned and directed the rebellion. Rwandan 'mid-level commanders' led the rebel forces and Rwanda had provided training and arms even before the rebellion began.[36] The Zairean Army fled before the highly effective rebels, looting and pillaging as they went. *Médicins sans Frontières*, whose familiarity with eastern Zaire pre-dated the 1994 crisis, reported that the Christian mission radio stations in the region went progressively off the air as the Zairean Army retreated and destroyed their radios.[37] With the French consul in Goma, MSF were the first to raise the alarm about the situation of the refugees in the camps caught between rebels and Hutu militia.

The eastern Zaire crisis internationalised conflict in the sub-region and added a new layer of complexity. The US Permanent Representative to the UN, Madeleine Albright, believed it to be as complicated a situation as any the Security Council had had to deal with. Between late October and December 1996, when Canadian Prime Minister Jean Chrétien acknowledged that there was no longer a need for the multinational force, the crisis highlighted three different facets of international responses to the region's problems:

- the impact of the humanitarian community;
- the difficulties of international military planning with mixed objectives, as against the effectiveness of a military campaign conducted by local players with their own agenda; and
- the disengagement from any political strategy, in the context of different Western interests, notably between France and the US.

There was a disposition in the more excitable parts of the French press to see evidence of an Anglo-Saxon scheme to develop, at France's expense, an arc of influence from Ethiopia and Eritrea via Uganda to Rwanda and Zaire. Gérard Prunier, the French historian of Rwanda and occasional consultant to the French Ministry of Defence, describes this as 'the Fashoda syndrome', with the whole world as 'a cultural, political and economic battlefield between France and the Anglo-Saxons'.[38]

UN officials in theatre predicted a catastrophe to rival the crisis of summer 1994. 'The aid was needed yesterday; the situation is shaping up to be "genocide by disease"', said MSF.[39] By 4 November, French Foreign Minister de Charette was lobbying the UN and allies for a humanitarian rescue mission. Prunier told the press that he had presented a plan to the French government suggesting a unilateral operation because 'we have the military capacity in Africa; we may have to forget about the rest of Europe and the UN because it would take too long'.[40] Prunier was right in his assessment of France's ability to take swift presidential decisions matched by equally swift deployments, but in the event President Jacques Chirac explicitly ruled out unilateral intervention. An African regional summit in Nairobi on 6 November asked the UN Security Council to take urgent measures to establish safe corridors and temporary sanctuaries by deploying a neutral force. African divisions on the Hutu–Tutsi issue were too great for a regional intervention to be credible, participants said privately; 'almost any African national contingent would be considered to be biased by one group or another'.[41] Mixed motives also applied in Europe:

> *Tutsis and the Zairean opposition blame France for backing President Mobutu and the former regime in Rwanda, while Hutus and even some French policy-makers see the Tutsis as protégés of 'Anglo-Saxon' powers (the US, UK and South Africa).*[42]

France pushed for an urgent UN mandate for a multinational intervention force of 5,000. The UK was cautious, but agreed at an Anglo-French summit at Bordeaux on 8 November to coordinate (the French version of the communiqué read 'to contribute to') efforts in the Security Council and the EU to help refugees in Zaire.[43] The UNHCR painted an alarming picture of the needs of the refugees, and other UN officials and some NGOs began to play to the spotlight: 'the West is willing to give money to others to clear up the mess but it will not send white bodies; it is something to do with the self-obsession of the 1990s'. Oxfam accused governments of failing to do their jobs and defaulting on their obligations under international law. Save the Children Fund (SCF), by contrast, argued against intervention, noting that access was possible and that the French were unacceptable in the region because they were seen as responsible for the situation.[44] On 7 November, Foreign Minister de Charette erupted:

> *I am knocking on people's doors asking, is anyone prepared to*
> *assume his responsibilities? The answer is 'could you come*
> *back tomorrow?' or 'we might lend an aircraft'. The main*
> *obstacle is the international community's spinelessness.*[45]

Washington, seen as the prime target of the Minister's attack, was not prepared to rush its fences in the immediate aftermath of the November 1996 presidential election. One official admitted that the scene was one of confusion, with proposals changing daily in an atmosphere of healthy scepticism about a humanitarian intervention; military planning was chaotic. The UK, moving cautiously towards a contribution if a mission could be demonstrated to make sense, preferred US command, but was prepared to accept 'lots of Americans bolted on'.[46] The Security Council adopted Resolution 1078 just before 2.00 am on 9 November, which, like Resolution 688 of 1990 relating to the Kurds, placed maximum stress on access and support for humanitarian organisations, but asked for an urgent report on arrangements for deploying a multinational force. The intervention lobby was unimpressed. EU Commissioner Bonino was scandalised:

> *The states who prevented a force being deployed are an*
> *international scandal, an international disgrace. The*
> *Security Council representatives should keep in mind that*
> *hundreds of thousands of refugees stranded cannot spend the*
> *weekend in Long Island as they do.*[47]

There was no force to deploy, nor indeed any mission; there was ignorance as to the need, the numbers and the whereabouts of refugees; there was unfamiliarity with the environment, with the rebels and their intentions, and disputes about leadership and the concept of the operations. Motives were mixed, although the White House spokesman was clear about US aims:

> *Even facing an urgent humanitarian situation, there is always a necessity for the commander-in-chief to have a clear focus on mission priorities, objectives, who participates, how the force would be structured, what the nature and duration of the mission would be, and how do you measure success and how do you get out.*[48]

South African President Mandela, under pressure to contribute, wanted clarification, asking 'but what is it that they want us to do'?[49] The Canadians offered to lead the mission; Lieutenant-General Maurice Baril, former UN military adviser, presented his case in Washington to command the multinational force. On 13 November, the UK announced its intention to make a military contribution and committed up to 1,000 troops on 14 November. On the same day, US Secretary of Defense Perry announced the US contribution. The mission would not be to disarm militants, nor to conduct any forced entry into the area, nor to police refugee camps; Goma airport and a land corridor back to Rwanda were the key. The UNHCR, the World Food Programme (WFP), Oxfam and Commissioner Bonino were concerned. The aim was surely to separate the militia from the refugees and preferably to disarm them.[50] Catherine Bertini, Director of the WFP, commented that if the camps were re-created on the same basis as before, then the force would have to come back in a year and repeat the exercise. The UN spokesman's attempt at compromise did not help:

> *This operation is by its very nature a humanitarian one and the international community is not going in to start a war. They are going in there to try to separate the militia from the real refugees; when you come to be fed, you don't need a gun. Some very useful ideas have been put forward on how to achieve separation without confrontation.*[51]

There had been no disposition to separate the militia from the refugees in 1994, and there was none again in 1996. The rebel leader, Kabila, made clear that he opposed any force that was not neutral –

by which he meant the French – and that in any case any force that came without a mandate to separate the *Interahamwe* from the refugees was infeasible, impractical and useless.[52] The other side of the argument was put from Goma by Mike McDonagh, Director of the Irish NGO, Concern, who told the press that 'if the rebels attacked the camps, they would dissolve. Despite the fact that some innocent people would be killed, the matter would be resolved for once and for all'.[53] By 14 November, the difference in views about the aims of the multinational force between participants and with and within the humanitarian community, were all too public. Even in France there was dissent. Pierre Messmer, a former Gaullist Prime Minister, commented caustically on the 'incredible campaign waged by the humanitarian community arguing that they faced the worst crisis since World War II'. Their analysis was faulty, they had exaggerated and lied, and it was clear that there was no catastrophe.[54]

Multinational force planning went into high gear from mid-November with Canadian, US and UK reconnaissance missions to the theatre. Having initiated the planning process, supported by US–Europe Command (USEUCOM), these key nations were inclined to judge for themselves the situation on the ground, as far as they could. A meeting of potential or actual troop contributors took place in New York to hear the report of the UN Special Representative, and at Stuttgart. The aim was to deploy about 8,000. Troops offered at this point included:

- about 1,000 US troops on the ground in Goma and a further 2,000–3,000 in neighbouring countries, including air-cargo handlers, medical personnel, civil affairs and psychological operations specialists;
- about 1,000 UK troops drawn from the Parachute Brigade and the Royal Marines;
- about 1,000 French troops;
- about 350–450 Spanish troops; and
- perhaps 100 transport or communications personnel from Ireland (then holders of the EU Presidency).

South Africa had still to determine the size of its contribution, Germany would not contribute and Belgium would help with training. Other Africans could deploy only if funding was available. In total, about 23 countries attended the general planning meetings. Former UN military adviser General Baril would command, with a US deputy – the French suggested that there should be three deputies, an American, a European and an African, but the UK was happy with a US deputy – and Entebbe would be the logistical base. The mandating Security Council Resolution 1080 was adopted on 15 November.

Within hours of the US announcement of Resolution 1080 on 14 November, Kabila and his rebel forces attacked the Hutu militia in the largest refugee camp at Mugunga a few miles north-west of Goma. The same day, French Foreign Minister de Charette expressed his fear to US Secretary of State Warren Christopher that the refugees would never have sufficient confidence to return to Rwanda.[55] On 15 November, however, an enormous outflow of refugees began to move across the frontier. About three-quarters of a million returned to Rwanda, of which between 100,000 and 200,000 were pushed north and west by the Hutu militants retreating with the Zairean Army.

Even in late November, Canada remained keen to proceed with deployment. After touring the area and meeting troop contributors, Baril announced on 24 November that the multinational force would facilitate the delivery of humanitarian assistance and the voluntary repatriation of refugees and displaced persons. The force would be politically and militarily neutral. Washington, following insistent telephone calls from Lionel Rosenblatt of Refugees International claiming that tens of thousand of refugees remained on the brink of death, was cautious. US National Security Adviser Anthony Lake gave his assurance:

> All I can tell you is that we will look at it day by day. And thus far every day we have seen movements that are encouraging. It is sorting itself out.[56]

The US Air Force and the Royal Air Force sent photo-reconnaissance missions over eastern Zaire to assess the numbers of the missing, and found three major centres where land and water appeared to be available. US military sources confirmed that over

600,000 refugees had returned to Rwanda and perhaps 200,000 remained. Bad feeling was created when UN humanitarian repres- entatives on the ground disagreed with these figures. Oxfam later accused the UK and US of 'airbrushing' 400,000 refugees from history,[57] while other humanitarian agencies disagreed and more pragmatically recognised that figures for a beneficiary population are often inflated. The UNHCR accepted that over 700,000 refugees had returned and perhaps around 100,000 remained in Zaire, driven onwards as human shields by the *Interahamwe* and the retreating Zairean Army. Only in March 1997 did some of these refugees emerge from the jungle, much enfeebled. The evidence for an acute humanitarian crisis between October and December 1996 was dubious. NGO claims of human-rights abuse by the rebels could not be verified, and donors had become wary of the public-relations machine.[58] But by May 1997, there was increasing evidence that there had indeed been substantial human-rights abuses against the remaining refugees by the successful rebels as they moved across Zaire to Kinshasa.[59] The debate was highlighted by Kabila's refusal to accept Roberto Garreton, the Chilean Special Rapporteur of the UN Human Rights Commission, to conduct an investigation in July 1996.[60]

The extent of the rebellion was difficult to judge at the outset. Regional rebellions had been stamped on in the past by Mobutu. Kabila's earlier revolutionary efforts in the 1960s had been unsuccessful and for over 30 years he had lived in obscurity. Was he autonomous, or a puppet with strings pulled in Kampala and Kigali? Not a military man himself, he operated in accordance with a calculated and coherent military strategy, as might have been applied by successful former rebel leaders such as Museveni or Kagame. A clever and swift campaign destroyed the stranglehold of the *Interahamwe* on the refugee camps obscured from public view, a task consistently shirked by the international community since 1994. Remarks by Claude Dusaidi, a close adviser to Major-General Kagame, and by Gideon Kayinamura, the Rwandan Permanent Representative, seemed to confirm the views of the conspiracy theorists by announcing that the return of the refugees rendered deployment of the multinational force unnecessary, and sensibly proposed that the funds be spent instead on peacebuilding projects in Rwanda to integrate the refugees.[61]

By mid-March 1997, the rebels had taken Kisangani and controlled one-fifth of the country. Kabila's early claims that he would march on Kinshasa had been taken as hyperbole. Initially, it was believed that the rebels were resolving the problem of the camps and creating a *cordon sanitaire* along the Burundian and Rwandan borders within an area only nominally under Kinshasa's control. But the rebel movement had picked up so much support from disaffected Zaireans as to threaten the survival of the Mobutu regime and to precipitate a row between France and the United States. Washington saw no need for a humanitarian mission when the bulk of the refugees had returned, nor was it inclined to prop up Mobutu and his regime. The French government continued to insist on a humanitarian mission until well into 1997, but its stance was questioned even by the French press, which doubted the government's humanitarian motives and regarded Mobutu as a lost cause.[62]

By mid-May 1997, the rebels were within 70 kilometres of Kinshasa. Suggestions from Paris, and briefly from UN Secretary-General Kofi Annan, that the multinational force might be resuscitated found no support. Appeals for a cease-fire from the Security Council had been ignored, and peace talks in South Africa and on a South African ship off the Congolese coast foundered as the architects of the successful campaign saw no reason to deal with Mobutu, only to topple him. The strategic situation had been transformed. Local action, skilled military planning and opportunism by Museveni, Kagame and Kabila turned into a clear local strategy and ultimately into a seven-month campaign that went far beyond tackling the instability of the Rwanda–Burundi–eastern Zaire borders to overturn the Mobutu regime. Major-General Kagame had served as head of military intelligence for Museveni's successful rebellion in the mid-1980s and had conducted his own highly sophisticated and effective campaign as head of the RPF in 1994. The intellectual derivation was clear in the use of psychology to drive the opposition forward and then to launch attacks on three sides, always leaving the enemy an exit. It was a classic example of the principle of minimum effort in war. Kagame admitted the 'link' with Kabila; Kabila in turn admitted to telephoning Museveni, his mentor, by satellite twice a week.[63] US influence, much rumoured in Francophone and press circles, was less clear, apart from the interest of professional diplomats in making contact with opposition elements to assess their nature. Similarly, the end of Mobutu's regime and his support for UNITA could only be a bonus for Luanda.

In April 1997, malnourished and pathetic, Hutu refugees had started to emerge from the forest. The UNHCR blasted the West for inaction as the press reported that 'the sick, the wounded and those too weak to walk are being left to die in the mud of the Zairean rainforest'. There were allegations of massacres and aid workers claimed the rebels in their successful advance were 'treating them [the refugees] like garbage'.[64] Kabila faced a public-relations disaster as he neared his goal. The debate about the Garreton appointment began to raise questions as to whether the victorious rebels were seeking to ensure that the Hutu killers of the 1994 genocide did not survive, even if there were civilian casualties in the process. The pressure shifted to political negotiations and a swift move to a transitional government in Kinshasa with real engagement and impetus from the United States.

Military Intervention Versus Political Reality

The conflicts of the African Great Lakes region between 1993 and 1997 were complex, interlinked and intractable, and presented difficult moral and political choices to the West. Genocide in 1994 was stopped not because of any Western intervention, but because of a brilliant, short campaign conducted by the RPF. With hindsight it is easy to suggest, as the former Secretary-General of MSF has done, that the West should then have given maximum support to the RPF. But the nature of the killing, initially perceived as civil war, was not apparent until late in the day, and the former government of Rwanda had powerful friends. In eastern Zaire, local action finally solved the problem of the refugee camps in a manner that an intervening force could not have risked because of the high collateral damage to women and children. Major-General Kagame, exasperated by the West's collective refusal to address so fundamental a security threat, made clear that if no one else would take action, he would. A clear goal bolstered by strategic opportunism and highly skilled military leadership, fuelled the campaign. But Kabila and his forces would be held accountable for the reported systematic killings of Rwandans presumed complicit in the 1994 genocide.

The multifarious proposals for external military operations during the period seem, in retrospect, the result of desperation rather than of a considered response following a clear political line. From late 1995 onwards, New York diplomats were bemused by UN Secretary-General Boutros-Ghali's constant reiteration of proposals that used the Former Yugoslav Republic of Macedonia (FYROM) as an example for deploying military forces in a preventive mode. Burundi was not comparable to FYROM. The OSCE and NATO policy of providing reassurance at state level through security dialogue – and the deployment of the UN Preventive Deployment Force (UNPREDEP) with US and Scandinavian forces should be seen in this context – was wholly different from the need to relieve the atmosphere of fear. Nor was peacekeeping or a preventive mission the obvious answer. The refusal of the UN to intervene militarily in Burundi was common sense rather than a failure of political will. In an internal conflict with a high degree of ethnic mobilisation, the choice is between taking sides and backing a winner – which will allow for a swift exit – or a major long-term commitment if the mandate is to be even-handed and protect civilians at risk. In violent domestic strife where there are no effective security forces, the intervener effectively takes over the role of the state and cannot leave until the state can provide that capability itself.[65]

The proposals for a humanitarian mission in Zaire were prompted by a combination of the new power of the humanitarian community and the need to offset the perception that the West was abandoning Africa, the weakest continent, to concentrate on its own problems: the future of European security; the Balkans; and NATO enlargement. Both of these forces pricked the conscience of the West into one of those 'spurts of inconclusive attention when crisis becomes intolerable' identified by Flora Lewis.[66] The UK, France and the US, all of which had launched and developed proposals to help build African capability to resolve its own problems, and who alone had the capacity to deploy to other continents within 48 hours, did not have the option to sit out a dramatic humanitarian crisis. Late-nineteenth-century politics of spheres of influence had left a legacy of division, particularly between the French and Anglo-Saxon worlds, which complicated the West's ability to work together. By May 1997, when the drama of the harried Hutu refugees in the

Zairean interior became clear, there was no external will to intervene.

The role of the humanitarian world in the crisis was instructive. From mid-1994 onwards, both Goma and Kigali had become cities under humanitarian occupation. Experts are familiar with the phenomenon of 'aid-worker syndrome', when field personnel come to identify fully with their clients. The humanitarian players beating the drum for a military intervention, led by Commissioner Bonino, France, MSF and Oxfam, contrasted with the pragmatic view of the NGO Concern that so long as there were no indications of widespread hunger or disease, the rebels should be left to clear the camps in their own way. Save the Children Fund commented:

> We have never called for an armed intervention; indeed we publicly question the usefulness of such a force. We have always maintained that the only lasting solution is a practical and political – and not a military – one which encourages the return of as many refugees as possible to Rwanda. Events over the past few days would seem to bear out the legitimacy of this approach.[67]

Yet even after the return of over 600,000 refugees, Commissioner Bonino was still accusing the world community of indifference bordering on racism: 'how many lives have to be in danger, how many people missing, to justify a deployment of troops by the civilised world?'[68] Given the highly political role played by some NGOs and the history of the multinational force, humanitarianism was increasingly seen locally as an arm of politics; this would play back into problems over access.

The dangers were apparent of responding to such short-term pressures, whether for an intervention force for Burundi or a multinational force for Zaire. The UK and the US were moved not by propaganda, but by their own

the dangers were apparent of responding to short-term pressures

analysis of what needed to be done and, more important, what should not be done, and by their ability to sustain the policy domestically. With regard to Zaire, UK and US sources consistently repeated the mantra of a short-term role and a limited and clear mandate. A military deployment would have changed dynamics on the ground. If it had come too early, the rebel attack on the camps would have been impeded and they would either have been re-established or relocated. Western forces would have faced the same ignominy as IFOR in Bosnia when militarily capable forces refused to take on police work in the camps, or were accused of doing nothing while local parties attacked civilians around them. The effect could have been a protracted commitment and to 'increase suffering by temporarily blocking events from reaching their necessary conclusion – a conclusion that sooner or later will come whatever the international community does'.[69] Nor were the UK and US prepared to instal the rule of law – or of Kinshasa – in an area that was recognisably already semi-autonomous. In the words of the *Washington Post*: 'Trying to save the country or teetering Mobutu regime from collapse is a mission beyond America's grasp'.[70]

In London and Washington in late 1996 there was something of a backlash against the humanitarian community when it became apparent that the refugees were neither starving nor dying, but were returning to Rwanda in relatively good condition. In the words of one US observer, 'no one wants to beat up on UNHCR but no one wants to drop troops in the jungle to find refugees who weren't even there in the first place'.[71] When it became apparent six months later that significant numbers of refugees were indeed in dire straits in the jungle, international attention was on the rebels' onward progress. There was no interest in intervention, now seen as a flawed proposal. The key in April and May 1997 was access for the humanitarian community and for human-rights monitors, as disturbing stories emerged of deliberate massacres of presumed *Interahamwe* as the rebels moved forward, and the UNHCR encountered a policy of calculated obstacles in organising returns to Rwanda.[72] Commissioner Bonino continued to claim that 'it was an international scandal' and that 280,000 refugees had still to be accounted for.[73] Long-experienced aid workers regarded a case based on arithmetical projections from the original beneficiary figure as a flawed basis for action.

Political reality makes it very difficult to launch a purely humanitarian intervention without the potential for wider and longer involvement. As Adam Roberts has shown, humanitarianism as a substitute for political action is not satisfactory; a view shared by the UN High Commissioner for Refugees Sadako Ogata:

> *The assistance and protection provided by UNHCR and its partners must not be used as a substitute for the decisive political and military action which is sometimes required to deter aggression, halt human-rights abuses and prevent mass population displacements.*[74]

A half-hearted military response without any underlying political action is a poor option. Governments may need to face up to the starker choices of supporting one side, to ensure a quick exit, or of a longer-term major commitment, whether to restore law and order or to protect civilians. Conflicts with a high degree of ethnic mobilisation last for generations rather than years, and are intense in their impact, particularly on civilians, as neighbours turn on neighbours. An intervention for humanitarian purposes in such cases becomes a major military commitment, and one of long duration.

The UN, like a successful corporation, must periodically adapt its product line to changing demands.
Former UN Under-Secretary-General for Peacekeeping, Kofi Annan, 1996

It is not that we do not care, but that we only care in bursts, so that policy becomes a series of last-minute rescue efforts. Thus it is now with Burundi.
Martin Woollacott, *The Guardian*, 27 July 1996

conclusions

Conclusions

As recently as 1994, anyone who predicted that the path from violent ethnic politics in Rwanda and Burundi would lead by mid-1997 to the collapse of Africa's 'most durable dictator',[1] and a seismic shift in power relationships in Central Africa would have received short shrift. UN High Commissioner for Refugees Ogata was most prophetic with her warnings from 1994 onwards that the Rwandan camps in eastern Zaire would fundamentally destabilise the whole region.[2] The preceding analysis of collective response has indicated that Western nations and the international organisations in which they worked were consistently wrong-footed by the complexity and pace of developments within the sub-region. The traditional tools of international diplomacy, from declarations and resolutions to sanctions, were difficult to apply to good effect.

In Burundi, proposals for a cease-fire, whether from the UN or the EU, were irrelevant unless coupled with efforts to tackle the core issues of insecurity, fear and the culture of impunity. Proposals for outside military intervention were so far-fetched as to be given no more than ritual support. Local sanctions enriched the power-brokers while the poor suffered. The political class in Bujumbura, denied an opportunity to play to the international audience from October 1996 when attention shifted to neighbouring Zaire, began to look inwards. A tentative process that could help promote trust between the parties began to gather pace, allowing San Egidio to facilitate direct talks in March 1997. The Kivu rebellion provided an opportunity, skilfully exploited, to treat the long-running issues of the refugee camps and border security. The calls for humanitarian military intervention in eastern Zaire in October 1996 were ill founded and distracted attention, both from regional dynamics and from the crisis in Burundi. An external 'humanitarian' operation to round up, protect and escort refugees – including genocidal killers – could only have been a major military commitment, with infinite potential for complication and long duration. Would the killers have been separated from the others? And if so, at what cost in terms of collateral damage? The danger was not of casualties to the interveners, but of ignominy.

Zaire had been on 'early-warning' lists for years as a fragile state whose collapse, without a clear successor regime to Mobutu, could precipitate widespread anarchy. When it emerged that the Zairean armed forces demonstrated no will to fight and that local communities embraced the rebels' progress, the uprising achieved an unexpected success, thereby fulfilling its goal without help from outside the region. The UN Security Council's call for a cease-fire in Zaire early in 1997 was directly inimical to the aims of the rebellion. The rebels had no interest in succumbing to pressures by US and South African negotiators, nor to the EU's terms for the nature of a new government during the final stages of the campaign.[3] The optimum would be an indigenous movement, capable and committed to effective governance.

Kabila's victory had been an 'African affair'

Kabila's indebtedness would be to his backers in the neighbourhood, not to the international community. The model could well be the Ugandan model of 'no-party democracy' rather than the multi-party approach favoured by the Europeans. Former President Nyerere understandably expressed his irritation with Western press comment to the effect that the US had supplanted French influence; Kabila's victory had been an 'African affair'.[4]

Enlightened outside support can be most valuable when an inexperienced government has just taken over. South African President Mandela gave his swift backing to Kabila after Kinshasa fell in May 1997 and, in a neat combination of statesmanship and economic self-interest, his Vice-President, Thabo Mbeki, immediately announced the despatch of a team of economic and financial advisers to help the new government in Kinshasa, and even suggested eventual membership of the Southern African Development Coordination Conference (SADCC).[5] Kinshasa would need to recognise that the natural economic and trade links of Zaire's eastern provinces lay to the south and east, and that the local autonomy Kabila himself had first sought could benefit not only Zaire, but Rwanda, Burundi and Uganda as well. Ugandan President Museveni and Rwandan Vice-President Kagame had both advocated sub-regional economic integration as the key to future stability.[6] President Mandela had also been a strong advocate of such integration for Southern Africa,

'we have predicted ten of the last three crises'

through the SADCC. Two powerful African strands were coming together politically, but sub-regional economic cooperation in any real sense could take longer.

It has been fashionable in the late 1990s to call for more early-warning and preventive diplomacy – a good example of the 'ideal', acutely difficult to carry through effectively. As the Bureau of Intelligence and Research (INR) at the US Department of State said in February 1997, 'we have predicted ten of the last three crises'.[7]

Lessons and Proposals
A UN Centre for Conflict Analysis
Before coherent response to conflict is possible, clarity and unity of understanding among key international players are essential. Most policy-makers live in a fast-moving world, and most will admit to having little time for in-depth reading. There are occasional targeted brainstormings and seminars – the US government, for example, had occasional meetings on Burundi and Zaire to brainstorm with outsiders. The UK Foreign and Commonwealth Office has held conferences, led by research analysts, that brought in academics and outsiders, for example on Burundi in late 1996 and on conflict management in southern Africa in April 1997. Paris sought advice from regional specialists before launching *Operation Turquoise* in 1994 and again in 1996. But beyond this, there is little willingness to bring outsiders into the charmed policy-making circle on a regular basis. Save the Children Fund makes a point of seeking expert academic advice before tackling a new mission; it believes that its activities cannot be divorced from an in-depth analysis of

local politics. An SCF conference on the Great Lakes in March 1997 commissioned papers and brought together experts from economists to demographers and political scientists, providing a good model.[8]

The problems of the African Great Lakes, like those in other internal conflicts, transcend single disciplines. Ethnic conflict is the field of the social scientist and the generalist. Illuminating recent work by academics such as Donald Rotchild, David Lake, Michael Brown, Stephen Stedman and Charles King should be required reading in foreign ministries and by all concerned with potential or actual conflict.[9] A practical proposal to counter the time pressures and to promote unity of understanding would be to set up a Conflict Analysis Centre within the UN Secretariat, possibly reporting directly to the Secretary-General. This would be responsible for policy analysis, not operations, and its success would be measured by the extent to which its work informed policy decisions across the world. It would require a dedicated Assistant Secretary-General, with good credentials as an academic and diplomat, at the centre of a team drawn from a variety of disciplines, including diplomacy, political science, the UNDP, the media, the military, business and psychology. Such a unit would provide the intellectual framework for policy response, whether by the UN, the OAU, NATO, the OSCE or the Association of South-East Asian Nations (ASEAN) Regional Forum (ARF) in a contact group.

the CAC would provide the intellectual framework for policy response

The Centre's advice would be independent; hence ideally it should be funded voluntarily by states and foundations, rather than from the UN regular budget. Indeed, a direct (not only funding) link with a respected external organisation could help protect the CAC from the normal push and pull of UN business. Structures would be light; the CAC would commission studies from acknowledged experts in whatever field it thought relevant. Conflicting points of view, not uncommon among academics, could be used to positive effect to establish the parameters of the problems. The Centre would:

- track academic work and policy responses, not least in the areas of future conflict;
- promote lessons learned, seminars and workshops;

- conduct a dialogue; and
- build good working relations with other international organisations and arrangements, including the OAU, the ARF, NATO, the World Bank and the EU planning cell.

The experience of skilled negotiators would be recorded and synthesised. Once its quality and links with other bodies were established, the CAC could supersede or at least inhibit some of the competition between international organisations that has been so marked a feature of international response to recent conflicts.

A Handbook of Lessons Learned

In order to assemble a box of policy tools, practitioners should know what to look for in internal and ethnic conflict, just as the counter-terrorism expert is aware of the core techniques of surviving in a hostage situation,[10] or as the instigator of a *coup d'état* is of the means described in Edward Luttwak's 'do-it-yourself guide' of the 1960s.[11] There are no templates for ethnic conflict, but a number of characteristics are commonly found. A UN Centre could synthesise experience in a study, which, regularly updated, could contribute to military doctrine. That local leaders are manipulative and untruthful is an elementary fact, mentioned by all negotiators in the Great Lakes region (and indeed in the Balkans). They know how to perform in front of the international media just as they do before the domestic audience. As a result, objective information fails to circulate, and rumour feeds on rumour. Civilians are used as pawns, and the fighters may not be members of any structured armed force, but civilians 'militia-ised' to support their own immediate territory. Humanitarian agencies are deliberately enticed in and then exploited for publicity, supplies and sometimes as shields for other objectives (military or political). Alternatively, the agencies may be denied access because of their increasing political role and media links.

Principles of international humanitarian law do not exist. Central control and a single strategic vision may be rare, especially in cases where small units may be fighting for their land. A number of local power centres may also control a more strategic resource – access to a river crossing or road (or tunnel, bridge and dam in Bosnia). Hence cease-fires are difficult to deliver; someone will be seen to win (usually the weaker side) and someone to lose. In former Zaire, a cease-fire before the fall of Kinshasa would have benefited Mobutu's forces. Cease-fires can be destabilising because local interests are threatened, or because, in an ethnic conflict, they do not deal with the problem of group insecurity. Agreements on cease-fires are usually preceded by an upsurge in activity to gain maximum advantage. Thus San Egidio, a team of experienced negotiators, argued for a cease-fire in Burundi not at the beginning, but at a later point in a process which began with restoring Constitutional and institutional order.[12]

Ethnic conflict or internal conflict with a high degree of ethnic mobilisation takes a long time to resolve – perhaps generations – and is particularly intense precisely because societies are ethnically mixed. Any intervention for humanitarian purposes in ethnic conflict, if premised on neutrality, will entail a long and substantial commitment. If, on the other hand, it comes to be seen as a commitment to protect one group against another, that essentially means taking sides. Hence the unarmed observer who poses no threat, like the OAU observers in Burundi, may sometimes be a better option. Taking over police functions and responsibility for law and order disempowers the state and is a further recipe for a long commitment. Ethnic conflict is evolutionary; moderates become marginalised or radicalised as options disappear. As a consequence of the 1994 Convention of Government, some Hutu abandoned FRODEBU and opted for armed struggle instead.[13]

Enhancing Abilities to Respond to Internal Conflict
Internal conflict is complex. Lessons that could be applicable from Bosnia to Burundi may fail to be learned or effectively used because of a lack of consistent cross-fertilisation within a foreign ministry, between military and civilians, or between organisations or governments and expert external analysts. The Scandinavians have developed a useful pattern of roving ambassadors for peacekeeping and for Africa. This enables the individuals to travel widely, learn by direct experience, maintain useful personal contacts with the NGO community, and be aware of developing lateral trends, whether on the ground or academically. US special envoys are traditionally more targeted on a country or a specific negotiation, for example in Mozambique. An EU special envoy, also sent to a particular area,

represents an embryonic common foreign and security policy, which has yet to prove itself operationally and may thus have less influence than an emissary from one of the major players, such as the UK, France or Germany. As UN SRSG in Mozambique, Aldo Aiello was able to draw on a trust fund from the Italian government, a key element in keeping the *Resistência Nacional Moçambicana* (RENAMO) in the peace process. EU procedures were less flexible when Aiello went as Special Envoy to the Great Lakes.

It has perhaps not been coincidental that Norway, not a member of the EU, has so regularly backed productive track-two negotiations. The Norwegian parliament directly assigns part of its aid budget to its Foreign Ministry for conflict management and activities related to peacekeeping. With a political ambassador with a wide-ranging remit freed of the need for traditional bureaucratic brokering on expenditure in foreign policy, Norway is able to respond swiftly, without publicity and to good effect, as it did in the Middle East and in Burundi through discreet funding for San Egidio. The model could be followed more widely.[14] The UK, in turn, since 1993 has developed a widely acknowledged model for 'peace-keeping training' jointly between the Foreign Office and the Army Staff College at Camberley. This is designed to break down communication barriers between, for example, military and diplomatic personnel, UN officials, NGOs and the media who might be present on the ground in responding to a conflict situation. They work together in groups, under pressure, to develop the mix of responses to a complex scenario.[15] Although national responses differ, key international players should be readier to draw in expert experience from outside, rather than to assume that their own colleagues have covered the ground.

Doctrinal Responses to Internal Conflict

In a situation like that in Burundi, projecting overwhelming force and air power does not deliver peace. Heavy manpower on the ground is needed to protect one group of civilians against armed attack from others in an ethnically mixed environment. This is unlikely to be available from the West. The complexity of a 'humanitarian intervention', as in eastern Zaire, may not be fully understood at the political level. Since there will be further such proposals, writers of military doctrine could usefully bring out the implications, in terms of large and long-lasting deployments, and the alternatives of taking sides by backing a local figure or of indirectly supporting local action. Another option may simply be to observe or 'bear witness'. Amnesty International reports, even on Burundi, have had an impact. Unarmed observers, such as those of the OAU or the UN human-rights monitors in Rwanda, may be better placed to inhibit generalised abuse than structured units, and tend to be more reliable than some of the less experienced NGOs. State-of-the-art communications of the kind used by journalists could offer some protection. Once a message has been despatched, the risks to the sender may be reduced. Media reports that undermine a warlord's image of himself can also have an impact. But the risks are high: in 1996, human-rights monitors were murdered in Rwanda and ICRC personnel were killed in Burundi; intimidation and harassment are common, and media equipment and money are regularly stolen. There are, however, individuals prepared to take such risks, and the possibilities should be considered in close consultation with field veterans.

Collaborating to Promote Policies for Peacebuilding

An imaginative plan for peacebuilding, reconciliation through reconstruction and economic integration throughout the sub-region – and allowing for the return of the remaining refugees – could be the key to stability in the African Great Lakes. Neither the UN nor the EU alone coped comfortably with the politics of overlapping internal conflicts. UN strength, with the OAU in support, could lie in gathering international backing for an overall peace settlement and in fielding a strong human-rights monitoring team for the entire sub-region. The UN family (including the UNDP, the Economic Commission for Africa (ECA) and the UN High Commissioners for Refugees and for Human Rights) should also work together with the World Bank to provide the analytical framework for a sub-regional plan encompassing economic development, an effective indigenous system of justice to end the culture of impunity, and the return of refugees.[16] Such a task-force-based approach should be standard practice and should be brought into play when the new Conflict Analysis Centre identified the potential for violent social conflict. In contrast to the somewhat aspirational aims of the EU and its continuing focus on emergency assistance during the period 1994–

97, real European strengths in terms of development aid, technical assistance and trade preferences could also support such a plan. Pending such a plan, donors should be able to deploy modest 'rapid-reaction finance' for immediate needs to help fragile governments create an effective judiciary and police force, financial and taxation structures and to start rebuilding a shattered economy. Whereas the conventional development agenda is slow and cumbersome, the Norwegian practice of giving its Foreign Ministry access to fast-disbursing funds for such primarily political purposes, and a new, more proactive approach within aid ministries in responding to such political considerations, could also encourage development institutions to accelerate their responses.

Conclusion

Between 1994 and 1997, key players in the African Great Lakes appeared to lose confidence in the West's commitment to help find solutions to their problems. Guilt over the genocide in Rwanda provoked a huge outpouring of humanitarian assistance rather than any political creativity in addressing the problem of the refugee camps and fundamental instability. Western attention was fitful and too often prompted by media interest, lapsing when the pictures were absent from television screens. Instead, a group of powerful leaders in the region demonstrated their clear determination to start setting the agenda themselves. Museveni, Kagame, Kabila (and even Meles) had long-standing ties and had all come to power by a military route. These were 'home-grown' solutions from decisive leaders. It may never be known whether Western, particularly US, powers provided any stimulus, or whether they merely turned a blind eye to the developments in Burundi, but certainly to see them as having been provoked by the US is misguided. Traditional Western patterns may be inappropriate here. Instead, non-party democracy and a strong element of sub-regional cooperation, politically and perhaps economically, may be the models for the future.

notes

Notes

Introduction

[1] Graca Machel, 'Impact of Armed Conflict on Children: Note by the UN Secretary-General', UN document A/51/306, 26 August 1996; UN High Commission for Refugees (UNHCR), *The State of the World's Refugees 1995* (Oxford: Oxford University Press, 1995).

[2] For the media's impact on policy-making, see in particular Warren P. Strobel, *Late Breaking Foreign Policy: The News Media's Influence on Peace Operations* (Washington DC: Endowment of the US Institute for Peace, 1997); Nik Gowing, *Media Coverage: Help or Hindrance for Conflict Prevention?* (Washington DC: Carnegie Commission, 1997).

[3] Donald Rotchild, 'Africa in the New Order', in Edmond Keller and Donald Rotchild (eds), *Africa in the New International Order: Rethinking State Sovereignty and Regional Security* (Boulder, CO: Lynne Riener, 1996), p. 11; see also Jane E. Holl (ed.), *Carnegie Commission on Preventing Deadly Conflict: Second Progress Report* (New York: Carnegie Corporation, 1996), p. 2; Stockholm Peace Research Institute (SIPRI), *SIPRI Year Book 1996: Armaments, Disarmament and International Security* (Oxford: Oxford University Press for SIPRI, 1996), pp. 15–21.

[4] See, for example, John Chipman, 'Managing the Politics of Parochialism', *Survival*, vol. 35, no. 1, Spring 1993, pp. 143–70; Michael E. Brown (ed.), *The International Dimensions of Internal Conflict* (Cambridge, MA: MIT Press, 1996), especially pp. 571–601.

[5] See Charles King, *Ending Civil Wars*, Adelphi Paper 308 (Oxford: Oxford University Press for the IISS, 1997).

[6] See Tom Woodhouse and Oliver Ramsbotham, 'Terra Incognita: Here Be Dragons. Peacekeeping and Conflict Resolution in Contemporary Conflict', paper delivered at the Initiative on Conflict Resolution and Ethnicity (INCORE) Conference 'Training and Preparation of Military and Civilian Peacekeepers', University of Ulster, Londonderry, 13–15 June 1996 (Londonderry: INCORE, University of Ulster, 1996),

especially pp. 13–16.

[7] Andrew Purvis, 'Looking Back with Hope', *Time*, vol. 148, no. 18, 28 October 1996, p. 36; and Diana Chigas, 'Preventive Diplomacy and the OSCE', in Abram Chayes and Antonia Handler Chayes (eds), *Preventing Conflict in the Post-Communist World* (Washington DC: Brookings Institution, 1996), pp. 25–97.

[8] The UN Special Representative of the Secretary-General (SRSG) in Burundi, Ould Abdallah, resigned in 1995 when the number of negotiators reached seven; it later reached 13. See also Stephen John Stedman, 'UN Intervention in Civil Wars: Imperatives of Choice and Strategy', in Donald C. F. Daniel and Bradd C. Hayes (eds), *Beyond Traditional Peacekeeping* (New York: St Martin's Press, 1996), p. 50.

[9] *The International Response to Conflict and Genocide: Lessons from the Rwanda Experience* (Copenhagen: Steering Committee of the Joint Evaluation of Emergency Assistance, March 1996), 5 vols, in particular Study 2.

[10] See the powerful analysis of the use of fear in ethnic conflict in David Lake and Donald Rotchild, 'Containing Fear: The Origins and Management of Ethnic Conflict', *International Security*, vol. 21, no. 2, Autumn 1996, pp. 41–75.

[11] UNHCR, *State of the World's Refugees 1995*; 'Burundi: Tanzania Expels 120 Tanzanian Refugees', Reuters Business Briefing (RBB), 11 January 1997.

[12] 'Chris McGreal in Muganga Uncovers the Crushed Militias' Blueprints for Battle', *The Guardian*, 18 November 1996, p. 11.

[13] See, for instance, David Rieff, 'Nagorno Karabakh: Case Study in Ethnic Strife', *Foreign Affairs*, vol. 76, no. 2, March–April 1997, pp. 128–29, which describes the impact of 'inflamed ethnic chauvinism combined with the memory of real communal suffering' breeding fantasies of original virtue versus enemy wickedness.

[14] Strobel, *Late Breaking Foreign Policy*, pp. 6–7; see also Nik Gowing, *Real Time Television Coverage of Armed Conflicts and Diplomatic Crises* (Cambridge, MA: John F. Kennedy School of Government, Harvard University, 1994), p. 87; Steven Livingston and Todd Eachus, 'Humanitarian Crises and US Foreign Policy: Somalia and the CNN Effect Reconsidered', *Political Communication*, vol. 12, no. 4, 1995, pp. 413–29.

[15] Kofi A. Annan, 'Peace Operations and the United Nations: Preparing for the Next Century', unpublished paper, February 1996.

[16] The European Union in particular has a tradition of action by declaration. See, for example, 'EU: CFSP Statement on Rwanda. Common Foreign and Security Policy Press Release', RBB, 12 April 1994.

[17] Reports emerged during June 1997 of consistent and brutal human-rights abuses as the rebellion progressed. See John Pomfret, 'Massacres were a Weapon in Congo's Civil War', *Washington Post*, 11 June 1997.

[18] Private interviews with academics and practitioners in Washington, New York, London and South Africa. The literature on the NGO experience is thin; NGO negotiators on the ground are often understandably reluctant to publish their experiences.

[19] These points had begun to emerge by mid-1997 in connection with the problems of implementing the 1995 General Framework Agreement for Peace in Bosnia and

Herzegovina (the Dayton Accord). See Julian Borger, 'Peace Troops Face "From Here to Eternity" in Bosnia', *The Guardian*, 22 May 1997, p. 14.

[20] Manoah Esipisu, 'Uganda: Multinational Force for Zaire Bides Time in Uganda', RBB, 3 December 1996.

[21] Alain Destexhe, 'The Third Genocide', *Foreign Policy*, no. 97, Winter 1994–95, pp. 3–17, especially p. 9; William Pfaff, 'Humanitarian Intervention vs Political Reality', *International Herald Tribune*, 18 November 1996, p. 8.

[22] In the former Yugoslavia, the EU, the OSCE, the Western European Union (WEU), NATO and Contact Groups all played a role between 1991 and 1996. In the African Great Lakes, the UN, the OAU, the EU, sub-regional groups and a number of individual states attempted mediation between 1993 and 1997.

[22] 'Peacekeeping' is used here as an umbrella phrase to describe the different facets of preventing and responding to a conflict in all its aspects; the term 'complex emergency', currently much-used by the humanitarian community, suggests a more limited reactive process.

Chapter 1

[1] See Michael E. Brown, 'Introduction', in Brown (ed.), *The International Dimensions of Internal Conflict*, p. 12; Lake and Rotchild, 'Containing Fear', p. 41; René Lemarchand, *Burundi: Ethnic Conflict and Genocide* (Cambridge: Cambridge University Press, 1996), p. xxviii.

[2] Michael Brown argues convincingly that most major internal conflicts are triggered by élite-level activities, in other words bad leaders. See Brown (ed.), *The International Dimensions of Internal Conflict*, p. 23. Rwanda and Burundi are good examples.

[3] There has been a wealth of scholarly analysis of ethnicity in Rwanda and Burundi. This is usefully summarised in Gérard Prunier, *The Rwanda Crisis: History of a Genocide 1959–1994* (London: C. Hurst and Co., 1995). See also Filip Reyntjens, 'Rwanda: Genocide and Beyond', *Journal of Refugee Studies*, vol. 9, no. 3, September 1996; *The International Response to Conflict and Genocide*, especially pp. 28–29; Lemarchand, *Burundi*; Jason S. Abrams, 'Burundi: Anatomy of an Ethnic Conflict', *Survival*, vol. 37, no. 1, Spring 1995, pp. 154–64; Ahmedou Ould Abdallah, *La Diplomatie Pyromane* (Paris: Calmann-Lévy, 1996); Agostinho Zacarias, 'Time to Stop a Genocide Culture', *The World Today*, vol. 52, no. 11, November 1996, pp. 286–89.

[4] Ahmedou Ould Abdallah, 'Genocide Is Not a Natural Disaster', address given at the Engles Conference Centre, Rotterdam, 10 October 1996, and private conversations with the author, Washington DC, 27 January 1997.

[5] René Lemarchand, 'Managing Transition Anarchies: Rwanda, Burundi and South Africa in Comparative Perspective', *Journal of Modern African Studies*, vol. 32, no. 4, 1994, p. 586.

[6] UNHCR, *State of the World's Refugees 1995*, p. 32; Lemarchand, *Burundi*, p. 172; Abrams, 'Anatomy of an Ethnic Conflict', p. 149.

[7] Lemarchand, *Burundi*, p. 63.

[8] See Lake and Rotchild, 'Containing Fear', pp. 41–75.

[9] Ould Abdallah, 'Genocide', p. 3;

Filip Reyntjens, *Burundi: Breaking the Cycle of Violence* (London: Minority Rights Group, 1995), p. 7.

[10] Lemarchand, *Burundi*, p. 98.

[11] *Ibid.*, p. 128.

[12] Letter of 25 July 1996 from the UN Secretary-General to the President of the Security Council, UN document S/1996/682, 22 August 1996, pp. 13, 42, 72.

[13] 'Rwanda: Rwandan Patriotic Front on Government Policy on Burundi "Government in Exile"', communiqué signed by Pasteur Bizimungu and broadcast by RPF Radio, 1 November 1993, in *BBC Monitoring Service: Africa*, RBB, 3 November 1993.

[14] Amnesty International, *Burundi: Armed Groups Kill Without Mercy* (London: Amnesty International, 12 June 1996).

[15] Declaration on the Great Lakes Region made by the Heads of State of Burundi, Rwanda, Uganda, United Republic of Tanzania and Zaire, Cairo, 29 November 1995.

[16] Private conversations with Judge Goldstone, Capetown, 28 October 1996, and with Ould Abdallah, Washington DC, 27 January 1997; Reyntjens, *Burundi*, p. 7; UN document S/1996/682, 22 August 1996, pp. 74–75.

[17] Letter of 7 April 1995 from the Permanent Representative of Burundi to the UN Secretary-General , UN document S/1995/278, 10 April 1995.

[18] Elias Canetti, *Crowds and Power* (Harmondsworth: Penguin Books, 1981).

[19] Report of the Secretary-General on the Situation in Burundi, UN document S/1996/116, 15 February 1996.

[20] 'Barundi' is the generic term for the Burundian people. Both forms are used in this paper.

[21] 'US Congress Panel Condemns Burundi Violence', RBB, 27 September 1988.

[22] 'FRODEBU Win 65 of 81 Seats: UPRONA Criticises Elections, Accepts Results', Radio Burundi, Bujumbura, in *BBC Monitoring Service: Africa*, RBB, 5 July 1996.

[23] 'Buyoya Calls for Peace in Independence Anniversary Speech', Radio Burundi, Bujumbura, 30 June 1993, in *BBC Monitoring Service: Africa*, RBB, 3 July 1993.

[24] 'Ndadaye Announces Amnesty', RBB, 12 July 1993.

[25] Pie Masumbuko, quoted in Elif Kaban, 'Burundi Ruler Defiant as Rwanda Joins Sanctions', RBB, 9 August 1996.

[26] Nicholas Kotch, 'Burundi's Tutsi Army an Anti-extermination Force', RBB, 26 July 1996.

[27] Private conversation with Charles Petrie, formerly an official with the UN Department of Humanitarian Affairs in Kigali and Bujumbura, 1994.

[28] Christine Shelly, 'US Condemns Coup', RBB, 21 October 1993.

[29] 'OAU Secretary-General in Rwanda Says that Something Has to be Done for Burundi', *BBC Monitoring Service: Africa*, RBB, 29 October 1993.

[30] 'Foreign Pressures Caused Burundi Coup – Museveni', RBB, 22 October 1993.

[31] 'Mandat pour la Mission au Burundi', internal UN document given to Ould Abdallah at the outset of his mission; Ould Abdallah, *La Diplomatie Pyromane*, gives a riveting account of his tour.

[32] 'Agreement Embodying the Convention of Government of 10 September 1994', circulated under cover of the letter of 8 March 1995 from the Chargé d'Affaires of the Permanent Representative of

Burundi to the UN Secretary-General, UN document S/1995/190, 8 March 1995.
[33] Conversation with Alastair Newton, UK government representative in Bujumbura 1996–97, London, 5 May 1997.
[34] Conversations with Catherine Watson, journalist and author, Kampala, 1 April 1997, and with Jan Van Eck, South African mediator in 1996–97, Capetown, 28 October 1996.
[35] Conversation with Ahmedou Ould Abdallah, London, 28 April 1997.
[36] Letter from members of the Security Council mission to the President of the Security Council, UN document S/1995/163, 28 February 1995; initial report on human rights in Burundi submitted by Special Rapporteur Sergio Pinheiro in accordance with Commission resolution 1995/90, UN document E/CN.4/1996/16, 14 November 1995, pp. 5 and 25.
[37] See Chapter 2 below for an account of the separate proposals for military intervention.
[38] 'Common Position of 24 March 1995 with Regard to Burundi', *Official Journal of the European Communities*, 985/91/CFSP, 1 April 1995.
[39] Conversations at Ministry of Cooperation, Paris, 1996.
[40] This is elaborated in Chapter 2 below.
[41] In Rotchild and Lake's view, a coalition of mediators creates the best mix of coercive and non-coercive incentives to overcome a stalemate. See Rotchild and Lake, 'Containing Fear', p. 70.
[42] Declaration on the Great Lakes Region.
[43] UN Security Council Resolution 1072, 30 August 1996.
[44] Private conversation with General Toure, Bamako, 13 August 1996.
[45] Stedman, 'UN Intervention in Civil Wars', p. 53; Rotchild and Lake, 'Containing Fear', p. 70.
[46] Philippe Lemaître, 'Propos Recueillis', *Le Monde*, 31 July 1997.
[47] EU Declaration by the Presidency on Burundi, 23 July 1996.
[48] Private report, Search for Common Ground, Washington DC, December 1996.
[49] Conversations with members of International Alert, London.
[50] Conversations with Vasu Gouden, Director of Accord, Capetown, June 1996; with Olara Otunnu, Director of the International Peace Academy, New York, February 1997; and with John Marks, President of Search for Common Ground, Washington DC, 28 January 1997.
[51] Private conversations with John Marks, President of Search for Common Ground, Washington DC, January 1997; with Kumar Rupesinghe, London, 1996; with UN officials and Western diplomats in Freetown and Abidjan, June 1996; and with Dr Miriam Mahiga, Bamako, Mali, August 1996.
[52] Paul Holmes: 'Mediators Details Burundi Peace Talks', RBB, 16 May 1997; 'Burundi: Presidential Press Statement Confirms Talks with Rebels', Burundi Press Agency, Bujumbura, 13 May 1997, in *BBC Monitoring Service: Africa*, RBB, 15 May 1997.
[53] 'Buyoya Says Reconciliation Talks Will Start Soon', Radio Rwanda, Kigali, 28 May 1997, in *BBC Monitoring Service: Africa*, RBB, 30 May 1997.
[54] Asfane Bassir Pour, 'Zaire – Washington Semble Désormais Déterminé à Mettre Fin à la Crise',

RBB, 11 March 1997.

55 See I. William Zartman, 'Dynamics and Constraints in Negotiations in Internal Conflicts', in Zartman (ed.), *Elusive Peace: Negotiating an End to Civil Wars* (Washington DC: Brookings Institution, 1995), pp. 7–8; King, *Ending Civil Wars*, pp. 71–74.

56 Chaim Kaufmann, 'Possible and Impossible Solutions to Ethnic Civil Wars', *International Security*, vol. 20, no. 4, Spring 1996, pp. 136–75, argues the case for separation.

57 Private conversation with Jan Van Eck, negotiator on Burundi, Capetown, 2 April 1997.

58 Private conversation with Major-General Kagame, Kigali, 1 April 1997; see also Save the Children Fund, *The Crises of the Great Lakes: Some Proposed Solutions* (London: Save the Children Fund, 1997), pp. 17–18, 94.

Chapter 2

1 Report on the Situation of Human Rights in Zaire, UN document E/CN.4/1997/6, 28 January 1997, pp. 26–27.

2 Report on the Visit of the Special Rapporteur to Eastern Zaire in July 1996, in *ibid.*, add. 1 of 16 September 1996.

3 See Michela Wrong, 'Weary Zaire Awaiting its Fate', *Financial Times*, 10 March 1997.

4 Charles Truehart, 'Special Envoy Says Peace Has a Chance', *International Herald Tribune*, 9 May 1997, p. 6.

5 Most of the group had known each other in exile in Dar es Salaam in the 1960s and 1970s.

6 'Great Lakes Summit Envoy Visits Bujumbura. Criticises UN Troops Plan', Burundi press agency, Bujumbura, 23 January 1996, in *BBC Monitoring Service: Africa*, RBB, 25 January 1996.

7 The phrase was used by Annan in 'Peace Operations and the United Nations' to describe the panoply of aid and sanctions measures that states can use against other states or leaders. Similarly, the UK and Europeans used positive and negative measures against the apartheid regime in South Africa in the 1980s.

8 Mark Huband, 'Burundi Blood-bath Runs its Course as West Looks On', *The Observer*, 31 October 1993; 'Oxfam Warns Burundi Faces Blood-bath Without Aid', RBB, 25 July 1996; Emma Bonino and Hervé de Charette quoted in 'EU Aide Says UN Zaire Inaction Is a Global Scandal', RBB, 9 November 1996, and 'Frustrated UN Envoy Leaves Zaire, EU Team Lands', RBB, 10 November 1996.

9 Allison Campbell of Care International quoted in Michela Wrong, 'Aid Agencies Ponder the Lessons of Eastern Zaire', *Financial Times*, 4 November 1996, p. 6.

10 The OAU's mission falls into the category of brave, but ineffective. Catherine Watson, a journalist in Bujumbura at the time, said the observers spent their time in discos with Tutsi girls; Ould Abdallah said they were tolerated by the army because they could be easily circumvented.

11 Conversation with Catherine Watson, Kampala, 1 April 1997, who reported from the bush with the RPF campaign and noted that colleagues recognised some of the same fighters around Kabila; Sam Kiley, 'Angola War Fear Rises as Tanks Go to Zaire Border', *The Times*, 9 May 1997, p. 15; 'Kinshasa Tense as Kabila Snubs Popular

Politician', *International Herald Tribune*, 24–25 May 1997, p. 1; James C. McKinley Jr, 'In Return for Aid in Fight, What Do the Rebels Owe?', *International Herald Tribune*, 23 May 1997, p. 6.

[12] Ould Abdallah, *La Diplomatie Pyromane*, p. 78.

[13] In Rwanda, Hutu northerners and extremists could not accept the substantial share of senior military posts awarded to the RPF under the 1993 Arusha accords. In Burundi, proposals to affect Tutsi dominance in the army provoked action in both 1993 and 1996; see 'Burundi: A Balancing Act', *Africa Confidential*, vol. 35, no. 13, 1 July 1994, p. 8.

[14] The description of 'collective rage' is from Lemarchand, *Burundi*, p. xxxi.

[15] 'Prime Minister Calls for Foreign Help', RTBF Radio 1, Brussels, 25 October 1993, in *BBC Monitoring Service: Africa*, RBB, 27 October 1993.

[16] Mark Huband, 'Burundi: Government in Hiding Drops Appeal for Intervention', *The Guardian*, 29 October 1993, p. 10.

[17] Thaddee Nsengiyareme, 'Africans Ready to Send Military Force to Burundi', RBB, 28 October 1993.

[18] Army spokesman Lt-Col. Jean Bosco Daradangwa, quoted in Deogratias Muvira, 'Burundi Army Rejects Foreign Troops – Spokesman', RBB, 1 November 1993.

[19] 'OAU Foreign Ministers Conclude Meetings in Addis Ababa', Egypt Radio, Cairo, 18 November 1993, in *BBC Monitoring Service: Africa*, RBB, 20 November 1993; talks at OAU headquarters, Addis Ababa, 19 August 1996.

[20] Evelyn Leopold, 'UN Official Says No to Peacekeepers for Burundi', RBB, 2 November 1993.

[21] Private conversation with Catherine Watson, Kampala, 1 April 1997.

[22] Ould Abdallah, *La Diplomatie Pyromane*, pp. 78–79.

[23] Evelyn Leopold, 'UN Official Says No to Peacekeepers for Burundi', RBB, 2 November 1993.

[24] Mark Huband, 'Government in Hiding Drops Appeal for Intervention', RBB, 29 October 1993.

[25] Private conversation with Ould Abdallah, Washington DC, 27 January 1997; Ould Abdallah, *La Diplomatie Pyromane*, p. 79.

[26] Report of the Secretary-General on the situation in Burundi, UN document S/1994/1152, 11 October 1994; letter of 29 December 1995 from the Secretary-General to the President of the Security Council, UN document S/1995/1068, 29 December 1995.

[27] UN document S/1996/116, 15 February 1996.

[28] UN document S/1995/1068, 29 December 1995; UN document S/1996/116, 15 February 1996.

[29] Press communiqué of the first Arusha regional summit on Burundi, 25 June 1996.

[30] Michela Wrong and Bruce Clark, 'Summit Stops Short of Using Force in Burundi', *Financial Times*, 1 August 1996.

[31] Joint communiqué of the second Arusha regional summit on Burundi, 31 July 1996; see also communiqués of the central organ of the OAU CRM, 5 August 1996 and 25 July 1996.

[32] Report of the Secretary-General on the situation in Burundi, UN document S/1996/887, 29 October 1996.

[33] Jane Standley, BBC World Service News, Nairobi, 6 March

1996; 'The Other War in Central Africa', *The Economist*, 14 December 1996, p. 67.

[34] When the Hutu extremists were chased from the refugee camps in Zaire in November 1996, their archives, discovered by the press, clearly implicated the Mobutu government.

[35] A local diplomat said that Tutsi from around the world, including the Banyamulenge, had joined the RPF in 1994 as part of a 'noble duty'; conversation with Major-General Kagame, Kigali, 1 April 1997; 'Zairean Rebels Have Complex Links across Region', RBB, 11 November 1996.

[36] John Pomfret, 'Rwanda Admits it Led Drive to Topple Mobutu', *International Herald Tribune*, 10 July 1997; Rwandan authorities made clear subsequently that the government's role had been purely supportive. See 'Kagame's Advisers Deny Report on Rwanda's Involvement in War in Former Zaire', Radio Rwanda, Kigali, 16 July 1997, in *BBC Monitoring Service: Africa*, RBB, 18 July 1997.

[37] Private conversation with Geoff Prescott, *Médecins sans Frontières*, Holland, 16 November 1996.

[38] Prunier, *The Rwanda Crisis*, pp. 104–8; Prunier, 'The Fall of the French Empire', *Wall Street Journal*, 24 January 1997; Alec Russell, 'France and US at Loggerheads in Struggle for Influence', *The Daily Telegraph*, 14 March 1997; Stephen Smith, 'La Débâcle du Régime de Mobutu et de la France', *Libération*, 14 March 1997.

[39] Mary Braid, 'UN Stalls over Zaire Nightmare', *The Independent on Sunday*, 10 November 1996, p. 2, quoting Dr Leslie Shanks.

[40] Ben Macintyre and Michael Evans, 'French Press for Intervention to Save Fleeing Hutus', *The Times*, 4 November 1996, p. 13.

[41] 'A Paralysed World Defers Action on Zaire', RBB, 6 November 1996.

[42] Leader, *Financial Times*, 8 November 1996, p. 17, which reflects perceptions on both sides of the Channel. Prunier, *The Rwanda Crisis*, pp. 104–5, gives an insider's view of the Fashoda syndrome and how it affects French policy-makers.

[43] 'Chirac, Major Agree Joint Efforts on Zaire Aid', RBB, 8 November 1996.

[44] Oxfam statement, 1 November 1996; Oxfam maintained an interventionist line. SCF's enthusiasm was more measured: it did not believe military troops would help. Neither did Care and Concern.

[45] 'France Disappointed by "Spineless" Zaire Reaction', RBB, 6 November 1996.

[46] Ian Black, 'Britain Agrees to Pitch in', *The Guardian*, 14 November 1996, p. 13.

[47] 'EU Aide Says UN Zaire Inaction Is a Global Scandal', RBB, 9 November 1996.

[48] 'US Expected to Join International Zaire Force', RBB, 13 November 1996; 'Africa-Bound US Troops Will Not Disarm Factions', RBB, 14 November 1996.

[49] 'Mandela Seeks More Details on Zaire Peace Forces', RBB, 9 November 1996.

[50] The 9 November 1996 UNHCR draft concept of operations was explicit on the need to separate the Rwandan intimidators and armed elements from the refugees.

[51] Ahmad Fawzi, spokesman to the UN Secretary-General, New York, quoted in 'Nations

Scrambling to Complete Plans on Zaire Force', RBB, 14 November 1996.

[52] Anthony Goldman, 'No Neat Military Answers to Messy Reality, Say Aid Workers', *Financial Times*, 15 November 1996.

[53] Mike McDonagh, Director of Concern, quoted in Sam Kiley, 'Hutus Trek North to Goma', *The Times*, 15 November 1996, p. 15.

[54] 'Un Ancien Premier Ministre Rejette l'Intervention Humanitaire au Zaire', Agence France Presse, 18 November 1996.

[55] Joseph Fitchett, 'Zaire Crisis Easing, France Takes Heat for Sounding Alarm', *International Herald Tribune*, 19 November 1996, p. 6; 'Rwanda Rejects Multinational Force for Zaire', RBB, 25 November 1996.

[56] Alan Cowell, 'Talks on Force for Zaire Bog Down', *International Herald Tribune*, 23 November 1996.

[57] Edward Mortimer, 'The Moral Maze', *Financial Times*, 12 February 1997, p. 24.

[58] Michela Wrong, 'Indecision Hits the Case for Intervention in Rwanda', *Financial Times*, 25 November 1996; Cowell, 'Talks on Force for Zaire Bog Down'; 'Aid Groups Tricked Britain into Airlift', *Mail on Sunday*, 17 November 1996.

[59] Stephen Smith, 'Des Morts sans Nombre dans l'Ombre de Kabila', *Libération*, 20 May 1997; MSF report, 'Dans l'Est une Stratégie Brutale d'Elimination', in *Libération*, 20 May 1997; John Pomfret, 'In Zaire, Tutsi Revenge Campaign Turned Sights on Mobutu', *International Herald Tribune*, 8 July 1997.

[60] Kabila finally accepted a UNDP official, Robin Kinloch, and promised to cooperate.

[61] James C. McKinley Jr, 'Refugees Exodus from Zaire Slows Down', *International Herald Tribune*, 18 November 1996, p. 1; James Bone, 'Rwanda Calls on UN to Disband Relief Force', *The Times*, 16 November 1996; 'Rwanda Rejects Multinational Force for Zaire', RBB, 25 November 1996.

[62] 'Triple Faillite Française', editorial, *Le Monde*, 19 March 1996; Smith, 'La Débâcle du Régime de Mobutu'.

[63] Conversation with Major-General Kagame, Kigali, 1 April 1997; James Walsh, 'Shaking up Africa', *Time*, 14 April 1997, pp. 36–42; Patrick de Saint Exupéry, 'Les Grandes Puissances sur la Touche', *Le Figaro*, 7 May 1997.

[64] David Orr, 'Thousands Left to Die as Zaire Airlift Begins', *The Times*, 2 May 1997, p. 19; Christopher Lockwood, 'Massacre of Hutus Casts Doubt on Kabila's Reputation', *The Daily Telegraph*, 1 May 1997, p. 23.

[65] In Haiti, where the problem was the weakness of state institutions rather than internal strife, experts estimated that it would take the UN ten years to train an adequate police force.

[66] Flora Lewis, 'With Election Over, US Should Turn to Africa's Problems', *New York Times*, quoted in *Sacramento Bee*, 11 November 1996.

[67] Letter from Mark Bowden, Africa Director, SCF, *The Times*, 23 November 1996.

[68] Leyla Linton, 'Racism Blamed For Apathy over Aid', *The Times*, 22 November 1996, p. 19.

[69] Pfaff, 'Humanitarian Intervention', p. 8.

[70] 'Washington is Right to Risk Another Misadventure in Africa', editorial, *The Washington Post*, quoted in the *International Herald*

Tribune, 16 November 1996, p. 6.
[71] Wrong, 'Indecision Hits the Case', p. 4.
[72] Conversations with Sadako Ogata and Sergio Vieira de Mello, UNHCR, Geneva, 21 April 1997.
[73] 'EU's Bonino Says Issue of Missing Refugees is "International Scandal"', RNE Radio 1, Madrid, 23 May 1997, in *BBC Monitoring Service: Africa*, RBB, 26 May 1997.
[74] Roberts, *Humanitarian Action in War*, pp. 79–88; UNHCR, *State of the World's Refugees 1995*, p. 125.

Conclusions

[1] Kevin Fedarko, 'Land of Despair', *Time*, 17 February 1997, pp. 46–47.
[2] See, for instance, UNHCR, *State of the World's Refugees 1995*, p. 32, which clearly encapsulates the views of High Commissioner Ogata from late 1994 onwards.
[3] 'EU Congo – European Union Stipulates What it Expects from New Authorities of Former Zaire', RBB, 24 May 1997.
[4] Afsane Bassir Pour, 'Zaire: Julius Nyerere – Le Transfer de Pouvoir a été une Affaire Essentiellement Africaine', *Le Monde*, 21 May 1997.
[5] Brendan Boyle, 'S. Africa to Keep Helping New Congo – Mbeki', RBB, 21 May 1996.
[6] Yoweri Kaguta Museveni, *Sowing the Mustard Seed* (London: Macmillan, 1997), pp. 185–86; private conversation with Major-General Kagame, Kigali, 1 April 1997.
[7] Private conversation at INR Bureau, Department of State, Washington DC, 30 January 1997.
[8] Save the Children Fund, *The Crises of the Great Lakes*.
[9] Lake and Rotchild, 'Containing Fear'; Stedman, 'UN Intervention in Civil Wars', pp. 40–63 ; Brown (ed.), *The International Dimensions of Internal Conflict*; King, *Ending Civil Wars*.
[10] 'Hostage Situations – Avoidance and Survival', guide prepared for UNPROFOR by experts from the Metropolitan Police, London, 1993.
[11] Edward Luttwak, *Coup d'Etat: A Practical Handbook* (London: Penguin Books, 1968).
[12] Paul Holmes, 'Italy: Mediators Detail Burundi Peace Talks', RBB, 16 May 1997.
[13] This section draws on King, *Ending Civil Wars*, as well as on visits to, and conversations with, practitioners in 13 or so peacekeeping missions and conflict zones between 1991 and 1997.
[14] Conversation with Ambassador Helga Hernes, Oslo, 6 January 1997.
[15] See Glynne Evans, 'The Challenge of Integrating Civilians and Military in Peace Support Operations', paper presented at the Lawrence Livermore National Laboratory, Livermore, CA, 10 September 1996; the exercise has been widely exported, to Africa and Australia among other places.
[16] The World Bank has been doing some thinking on emergency reconstruction assistance, but still seems reluctant to enter into substantive dialogue with key players such as the UN, the ECA and the OAU.